Tiptoeing to windows and tapping on doors, Harriet whispered that the train to freedom would be leaving that night.

Did anyone want to get on board? Yes! Again and again, the excited answers came back. Yes! By the time the moon was high, a large group had gathered at the dark end of the fields by the road . . . Harriet led the slaves across the road, into the woods, along the old path, and north to freedom.

A Background Note about
HARRIET TUBMAN: Freedom Leader

In 1850, there were more than three million slaves in the United States. Many of them had been so badly beaten and mistreated that they had given up all hope of ever being free. But Harriet Tubman never gave up hope. Even as a child, Harriet knew that slavery was wrong and cruel. Though her parents begged her to show respect to her master, young Harriet refused. And as soon as she heard about the North Star and freedom, Harriet's life's mission was set into motion.

This is the story of the fearless woman who led hundreds of slaves to freedom along the secret paths known as the Underground Railroad. Harriet Tubman ran away alone in 1849. Then, for the next ten years, Harriet returned to the South again and again, gathering up groups of slaves and showing them the way to freedom.

Many people only associate Tubman with the Underground Railroad, but during the Civil War, Tubman worked long hours in Army hospitals caring for wounded soldiers. She also wore a Yankee uniform, carried a rifle, and worked as a spy. Sneaking through swamps and backwoods, Harriet uncovered important information that helped win many battles.

Today, we celebrate Harriet Tubman Day every year on March 10th—the day Tubman passed away in 1913 at the age of 92.

HARRIET TUBMAN:
Freedom Leader

Tanya Savory

TP THE TOWNSEND LIBRARY

HARRIET TUBMAN:
Freedom Leader

TP THE TOWNSEND LIBRARY

For more titles in the Townsend Library,
visit our website: **www.townsendpress.com**

Townsend Press Inc.
439 Kelley Drive
West Berlin, NJ 08091
cs@townsendpress.com

ISBN-13: 978-1-59194-101-9
ISBN-10: 1-59194-101-6

Library of Congress Control Number:
2007941664

CONTENTS

CHAPTER 1

"*What* is this?" screamed Miss Susan to seven-year-old Harriet. Miss Susan, as the slaves were told to call her, had run her finger along the top of the dining room table. It had picked up dust.

"Answer me, you little brat!" It was the fourth time Harriet had tried to dust the furniture. She had done exactly as she was told, but for some reason she kept doing it wrong. And every time she did it wrong, Miss Susan grabbed the rawhide whip above the fireplace and beat her. Now, she was reaching for the whip again.

"But Miss Susan," Harriet pleaded, her voice shaking, "I done swept and dusted just like you told me. I . . ." But it was no use. The whip was already cutting into her skin, leaving marks that would last the rest of her life.

"You are doing this on purpose just to be bad!" Miss Susan shouted as she hit tiny Harriet again and again. "No one could possibly be so stupid. Not even a slave child!" Miss Susan had taken Harriet from her original owner just that morning. She would try her out for a week first to see if she wanted to buy her. So far, things had gone terribly.

Suddenly, Emily, Susan's older and kinder sister, burst into the room.

She grabbed the whip from her sister's hand and said, "If you do not stop whipping this child, I will leave this house and never come back!"

Miss Susan stomped out of the room and slammed the door. Emily sat down and quietly asked Harriet to tell her exactly how she had dusted the room. Between sobs, Harriet explained that she had swept the floor and then immediately dusted the furniture just as she was told to do.

"But Harriet," Emily asked gently, "Didn't you wait for the dust from sweeping to settle first—just like you do when you dust at your home?"

Harriet looked up at Emily through her tears, not sure of how to answer this strange question. "At home? No ma'am. Ain't no nice tables and such to dust. Just nine blankets on the dirt floor for my brothers and sister and me."

Emily sighed and rested her hand on Harriet's trembling shoulder. The poor child really didn't understand. Emily hated the cruel way slaves were treated—particularly children. But this was 1827 in southern Maryland, and the whip ruled when it came to slaves, young or old. After patiently explaining how to dust, Emily placed the whip back above the fireplace, praying silently that it would not be used again on this little girl.

But much later that night, Harriet found herself in trouble once more. Even after a 15 hour day of cleaning and helping in the kitchen and gathering firewood outside in the cold, seven-year-old Harriet was put in charge of Miss Susan's infant son.

"And I'd better not hear a single sound from him," Miss Susan said, "or you'll be whipped for the fifth time today." With that warning, Miss Susan went to bed in the next room, the rawhide whip beneath her pillow

Exhausted and terrified, Harriet did the best she could do. She rocked the child in the dark for hours, but Harriet finally nodded off. When the rocking stopped, the baby began crying, and Miss Susan rushed into the room with the whip.

After only a few days of this, Miss Susan returned Harriet to her original owner, Edward

Brodas, claming that Harriet was too stupid and too lazy to buy. Mr. Brodas was angry about having a worthless slave returned to him, but Harriet was thrilled to be back home with her family and friends.

Harriet was particularly close to her father, Ben, whose own mother and father had been tied up in chains with many others and brought to America on a ship from Africa many years earlier. After dinner on Saturday nights, Daddy Ben would often tell the story his father had told him. The first night that Harriet (or "Hat" as her family called her) was home, her father told the story again.

"The slave traders kidnapped at least 500 of 'em," he'd begin. "Then they were all chained together in the very bottom of a huge ship with no sunlight for weeks and weeks. Ain't no room to move or lie down or barely breathe all that time. Smelled something terrible, and everyone was so scared and hungry and sick. Nearly 100 of them died before they reached Charleston Bay. But not my mama and daddy."

Ben paused and looked proud, angry, and sad all at the same time. Harriet quietly went over and sat in her father's lap, putting her small hand on his.

"But why didn't they try to run away from those slave traders?" Harriet asked.

Harriet's father looked at her for a long time

and shook his head sadly and said, "I suppose some tried, Hat. But if they were caught, they knew they'd be beaten and maybe killed. I reckon they were too afraid to even try."

Harriet gazed into the fire wondering if she would have been too afraid to try and escape. Just before drifting off to sleep, she whispered, "I would have run."

The next morning, Harriet woke up early. Her mother, Rit, was calling her name and telling her to get up and get ready. Get ready for what? Harriet wondered. She rolled over to see her sister and seven brothers still all sound asleep on the cabin floor. They were wrapped up in old blankets worn raggedy with use. Their beds were little piles of straw spread over the bare dirt floor. Harriet sat up and stared into space for a couple minutes. She was trying to remember a horrible dream she had been dreaming. In it, hundreds of black children walked in single file down a dark road. They were chained together at their ankles and their necks, and many were crying and bleeding. Beside them walked a tall white man with a whip in his hand.

"Hat! Hurry it up. You're going over to the Big House this morning," Rit called from the front room.

The Big House? A cold shiver went down

Harriet's back. "The Big House" was where her owner, Master Brodas, and his wife, Miss Sarah, lived. Being sent there usually meant you were either being sold or you were in trouble. Harriet pulled on her little dress—an old burlap feed sack with holes cut for her arms and head, but it was the only "dress" Harriet had ever known. She ran into the other room with a frightened look on her face.

"Why, Ma? What did I do? Master Brodas ain't selling me down South, is he?" Harriet had heard some terrible stories about the plantations far away in South Carolina or Louisiana where slaves did backbreaking work in cotton and rice fields. Down there, the masters were cruel and dangerous, and the bugs were huge and deadly.

"No, Hat. Nothing like that." Rit was smiling. "Miss Sarah needs some help and she says she figures you was just being stubborn with Miss Susan, and so she'll give you another chance. You get to work in the Big House!"

"But . . . ," Harriet began. She knew her mother wanted her to have an easier life than working outside on the Brodas's farm. It was considered better and easier work to be in the Big House, but Harriet dreaded the thought of dusting tables and rocking babies again. She'd rather be slopping the hogs or working in the fields with her brothers.

"No 'buts,' Hat." Rit was already handing her some cornbread and scooting her out the door. "You're nearly eight years old. Too old to be at home not working. So don't you get in trouble this time or Master Brodas is likely to sell you off far away."

Harriet sighed and began walking up the hill to the Big House. At least she would be with her family at night. Maybe Miss Sarah would be nicer. And maybe she didn't use or even own a whip. Harriet said a little prayer in her head as she knocked on the back door used only by the slaves.

A very old slave named Mary who worked as the cook opened the door and glared at Harriet for a moment. Then she pushed her toward the kitchen with, "Miss Sarah say you work in the kitchen today." After that, Mary barely spoke to Harriet except to grunt out orders to peel potatoes, pluck chickens, chop vegetables, or gather firewood. At one point, Harriet drew up enough courage to ask Mary whether or not Miss Sarah owned a whip. Without even looking Harriet's way, Mary barked, "You fixin' to find out if you keep askin' stupid questions." After that, Harriet worked in silence.

Around 2:00, the meal for Master Brodas and Miss Sarah was ready to carry out to the long, oak dining room table. While Mary piled the food onto silver and gold serving dishes,

Fred (the Brodas's butler) and Harriet carefully brought food to the table. Harriet could not believe that such incredible amounts of food could be eaten by two people. Plus, she had never seen many of the foods she carried out: a cake with fluffy frosting, gravy, and mashed potatoes with lakes of butter. And one small bowl in particular was irresistibly intriguing to her—a bowl full of sugar cubes. Harriet had never even tasted sugar, but she had heard about it.

Master Brodas and Miss Sarah came into the dining room arguing about something having to do with the baby. Harriet and Fred stood still at the far end of table awaiting any orders from Master. But Harriet's eyes were glued to the sugar bowl. It was within reach, and both Master's and Miss Sarah's backs were turned to her as they continued to argue. It would be so easy . . .

In a split second, Harriet snatched a cube out of the bowl. And in that very second, Miss Sarah spun around and caught her.

"WHAT are you doing?" Miss Sarah yelled at Harriet. Harriet stood frozen, the sugar cube still gripped tightly in her small hand.

"Fred," Miss Sarah said, her eyes burning with anger, "bring me my whip. I will not have my slaves, my property, stealing from me!" She began walking toward Harriet slowly, pointing her finger at her and saying, "You are in big trouble, little girl."

Harriet let the sugar cube slide slowly out of her hand and onto the floor with a little tap. As Miss Sarah got closer, Harriet could think of only one thing—Run! Suddenly, she was flying through the kitchen, out the back door, and across an empty tobacco field in the cold October afternoon. Behind her, she could hear the fading screeches and threats of Miss Sarah and the running footsteps of Master getting closer. Harriet did not slow down. She ran with every bit of strength she had until, finally, Master's footsteps began to fall further behind her.

Harriet ran until she was on the far side of the farm near the pigpens. Without a second thought, she scurried under the fence and slid into the deep pig mud. No one would think of looking for her here! As she lay still, trying to catch her breath, she felt as though someone or something was staring at her. Slowly, she lifted her mud-covered face. Only a couple feet from her was a giant sow, three times the size of Harriet, and the sow definitely did not look pleased to have found a little girl in her pen. Harriet knew that mother pigs could be dangerous, so she carefully slid away from the sow and huddled on the other side of the pen.

Harriet lay still in the mud for hours. The moon rose, owls called back and forth, and Harriet did not move. All night, she listened for the sound of Master's footsteps. Just before dawn, shivering with cold, she curled up next to several smaller pigs and fell asleep for a few hours. But she awoke in a panic to the sound of a voice and clattering metal. Ducking behind a pile of muddy hay, Harriet listened, her heart beating wildly. But it was only the old half-blind slave, Peter, coming to throw slop to the pigs. One, two, three buckets of leftover food and garbage were tossed into a long trough for the pigs. Then Peter was gone.

Cautiously, Harriet crawled toward the trough. She was very hungry, and some of the slop looked good enough to eat. In fact, much of it was food that Harriet had helped prepare the day before! Harriet squeezed in among the smaller pigs for her share. *These pigs eat better than I do,* Harriet thought bitterly as she ate.

All that day, Harriet hid in the mud and hay, coming out now and then to eat slop. After a while, the pigs ignored her, and even the huge sow (who Harriet decided looked quite a bit like Master) was no longer watching her. Twilight came, and the first stars came out. In the distance, she could hear some slaves singing, and she wondered if her family was worried about her.

Some time much later, Harriet awoke with a start. Footsteps! They came closer and closer. Harriet did her best to hide between the pigs, but the steps seemed to be coming right to her. Suddenly she looked up to see the outline of a tall man. He was holding something that looked like a whip in one hand, and he was reaching down to grab her with his other hand.

CHAPTER 2

"Harriet!" A low voice whispered her name as a big hand grasped her and began yanking her out of the pig mud. Harriet let out a short, startled scream.

"Hat, hush! It's me. Be quiet now."

"Daddy?" Harriet reached up to touch her father's face in the dark and then breathed a long sigh of relief. What she had thought was a whip was only her father's old walking stick.

"You in a world of trouble now," Ben said as he wrapped her in a blanket and settled her against his shoulder for the long walk back to the cabin. His voice sounded sad and very tired. Harriet wondered how long he had been searching for her.

"But how did you find me?" Harriet asked.

"Old Peter may be nearly blind, but he

knows when there's a little girl hiding in a pigpen," her father said with a laugh in spite of his worry. "I had to wait until now to come get you so nobody'd see me."

Both Harriet and her father were quiet for a long time as he carried her home. Finally, Harriet whispered in a shaky voice, "Is Master gonna sell me down South now, Daddy?" Harriet's fear of being sold to an even crueler master and being sent far away from her family was much greater than her fear of the whip.

"Don't know about that yet," her father answered. "But I do know that you gonna go first thing tomorrow morning to say you're sorry to Miss Sarah. And then you've got to take the beating coming to you. It's the only way. You've done something very wrong, and you have to pay the price."

Harriet tightened her grip around her father's shoulder. Done something very wrong? Pay the price? Even at only seven years old, Harriet sensed how horribly unfair all of this was.

"Miss Sarah can hit me all she wants, but I ain't saying I'm sorry," Harriet snapped angrily.

"Now listen to me," her father said sternly as he set her on the ground, placed both hands on her shoulders, and looked into her eyes. "You can't be so stubborn. Don't you know that slaves get beaten even worse for being stubborn?"

"Don't care," was all Harriet said. Then she turned and ran the rest of the way home.

The next morning, Harriet walked slowly up to the Big House to receive her punishment. Miss Sarah had gathered all the slave children together to watch Harriet's beating so that it might teach them all a lesson about what happens when a slave child steals or lies. The children, some as young as three, stood close together holding one another's hands. Some of the youngest children were crying silently. All of the children were shaking.

True to her word, Harriet would not apologize, and this only made the whipping worse. But Miss Sarah seemed satisfied with the fear she saw on the other children's faces. They were also witnessing what happens when a slave refuses to apologize. Finally, Miss Sarah threw her whip to the ground in disgust and motioned for all the children to leave.

"And you," she said, pointing to Harriet who lay on the ground bleeding, "you are too stupid and too dishonest to work in my house. You had your chance, and you won't receive another one. You can just work in the fields with the boys. That's all you're good for." With that, Miss Sarah slammed the front door, leaving Harriet to crawl back home.

For three days, Harriet fell in and out of consciousness as Rit tended to her wounds and prayed that her daughter would learn to obey the rules and be a humble slave who bowed down to her master. Rit had seen more than a few slaves, both men and women, killed or tortured for "crimes" no worse than what Harriet had done. Once, she had seen a young female slave's fingers cut off on her right hand. This was the punishment for taking a bottle of milk from her master in order to feed her hungry children.

But as Harriet slept, strange dreams and visions drifted through her mind. She saw a bright star that seemed to be asking her to follow it. She saw a line weaving through a distant land. And on the other side of the line were kind white people who reached out their arms to her to help her across to safety. But Harriet's dream of crying children chained together also haunted her. So as she recovered from her beating, Harriet prayed too: *God, make me strong and able to fight.*

Within a week, Harriet was in the tobacco fields with her brothers. She preferred it to cleaning and cooking, but it was terribly hard work. From sunrise to sunset, little Harriet chopped weeds and hauled sacks of tobacco to carts. At the end of every day, she was so tired that she could barely eat. In the mornings, she was often so sore that her brothers would have to help her walk back out to the fields.

But as the months and then the years passed, Harriet grew stronger and stronger. In fact, by the time she was in her early teens, she had grown so strong that her master began showing her off to his friends.

"You there. Harriet!" Master Brodas called to her one afternoon from the edge of the field. "Come here and lift this bale. I got a bet on you."

Harriet slowly moved toward Master Brodas and three other men who were standing in a circle smoking cigars and drinking something out of a silver flask. Harriet had not grown into a pretty teenager. She was barely five feet tall with drooping eyes and a scowl. The men all looked at her for a moment and then burst out laughing.

"That's right, gentlemen," Brodas said with a piggish grin. "She may be short and ugly, but she's stronger than an ox. Y'all lay down your money if you don't believe she can lift this here hundred-pound bale."

The men sized Harriet up and down, and one even walked over and felt her arms and slapped her legs. *I ain't no more than some animal to them,* Harriet thought angrily. *I'm a human! Not some ox trained for their games.*

"All right then, now, girl, pick up that bale. Don't make me ask you again," Master Brodas snapped.

In a quick and easy movement, Harriet lifted the bale chest-high and then threw it back down harder than she needed to. The men all clapped and whooped, but Harriet neither smiled nor met their eyes. *Ain't gonna give them the satisfaction of even looking their way,* Harriet thought as she immediately turned her back on the men and returned to the field.

"You mind your attitude, girl!" Brodas shouted angrily. But Harriet refused to acknowledge the man she was forced to call "Master." She just walked on, her head held high.

Life on the plantation was not all work and humiliation for Harriet, however. From her earliest days in the fields, she had discovered something magical and wonderful that she loved: singing. Every morning, as the sun was barely peeking over the laurel trees and the birds began to fill the pink skies, a low humming from the slaves would begin out in the fields. It would grow deeper and richer, full of a hundred different voices. It was a sound so sweet and real that Harriet was sure that it was what heaven must sound like.

Suddenly, a single deep voice would pierce through the humming of the slaves and sing out:

> *Go down, Moses,*
> *Way down in Egypt's land.*
> *Tell old Pharaoh,*
> *Let my people go!*

On "Let my people go," all the voices would join in together in a thunder that Harriet would never forget. Before long, Harriet had learned all the words to "Go Down, Moses" and sang along in her rich, low voice.

Still, the song sometimes troubled Harriet. She knew the Bible story about how God had punished Pharaoh for having slaves. She knew that Moses had helped fight Pharaoh and free the slaves. But what about now? Why didn't God punish Master Brodas? Where was the Moses for her people? Would no one fight for them? Finally, one hot Saturday evening, Harriet heard some talk that both scared her and gave her hope.

"I'm telling you that Nat Turner killed his master! Says so right here." The voice came from a slave named Zeke. Zeke was bent over a newspaper on a low table in his cabin. Nearly thirty slaves, including Harriet and her father, were packed into the cabin.

"Slit his throat and then killed the rest of

the family in the middle of the night," Zeke said, nodding.

"You making that up. No slave ever killed a white man!" a voice protested from the back.

"I am NOT making this up!" Zeke pounded his fist on the table and pointed to the paper. "Says right here: 'Nat Turner and his group of twenty other slaves slaughtered his master and his master's wife and children. They then went from door to door killing every white person they could find. At least fifty white people in southern Virginia were killed.'"

An uneasy silence filled the cabin. Zeke was the only slave on the plantation who could read. So what he was saying must be true. Groups of slaves would often come to his cabin on Saturday nights to hear the news of the week. But this had to be done in secrecy. It was illegal for a slave to know how to read or write, and Zeke could be killed if Master Brodas found out.

"But . . . but where will he go now?" a low voice asked nervously. Everyone in the cabin turned to see who had spoken. It was fourteen-year-old Harriet.

"Reckon he'll follow that North Star to freedom and take his twenty friends along if he knows what's good for him," Zeke said with a frown.

"North Star? To freedom?" Harriet asked.

"Child, ain't you heard the talk?" an old woman spoke up. "Every day now, there's slaves running away by night and following that bright star at the end of the Little Dipper's handle. Why, you can follow it all the way up to a line you cross where there ain't no more Master! White people are nice as they can be once you cross that line."

Everyone in the cabin then began talking excitedly about freedom and Nat Turner and the North Star. But Harriet sat very still, thinking very hard. *So it is possible to run away! That's what the star and the line in my dream all those years ago meant. God has given me a sign . . .*

But in the middle of her thoughts, Daddy Ben leaned close to Harriet and grabbed her arm so tightly it hurt.

"Don't listen to them, Hat. Don't even think about it," he whispered fiercely. "It's too dangerous! Runaway slaves are hunted down and hanged from trees or beaten to death. Your freedom ain't worth your life, Hat!"

But Harriet wasn't listening to her father. She pulled her arm from his grasp and slowly walked out the cabin door. Standing in the little dirt yard in front of Zeke's cabin, Harriet stared up into the wide heavens. Raising her hands up, she let her fingers find the stars of the Little Dipper and trace down the Dipper's handle. There, at the very bottom, was the brightest star in the sky. Harriet's heart raced. With tears

HARRIET TUBMAN: FREEDOM LEADER **21**

in her eyes, she whispered a promise to herself: "I don't know when and I don't know how yet. But one day, I'm gonna follow that star."

Several weeks later, a group of slaves huddled in the candlelight of Zeke's cabin once again. There had been whispers through the fields that day that something very bad had happened.

"Oh, Lord," Zeke said, mostly to himself as he leaned in close to the newspaper he had stolen from Master's trash. The cabin was utterly silent as the group waited for Zeke to read out loud to them.

"Just horrible," Zeke commented and shook his head as he continued reading silently. There were a few sighs around the cabin and someone was tapping a foot. Harriet, as impatient to hear the news as anyone, wished more than anything that she could read. *Master don't want us to read, 'cause then we'd know as much as him. Even more!* Harriet thought angrily.

"Unbelievable," Zeke mumbled to himself.

"Oh for heaven's sake, Zeke! Read it out loud! We all want to know what's going on," a voice boomed from the back.

Zeke jumped a little, pulled off his cracked glasses, and wiped his eyes. He looked around the room sadly.

"Well," Zeke began, "says here that they done caught all of Nat Turner's group a few weeks ago. Killed all twenty of them. Nat broke free and hid out in a cave for a while, but then they found him too."

There was a long pause before Zeke continued.

"Says here that they hanged him and then," Zeke sighed and rubbed his eyes, " . . . then they cut him up into little pieces and skinned him. Seems as though white people is buying bits of him to remind us slaves what happens if we try to hurt a white man. Or run away."

Harriet felt sick to her stomach. Everyone began talking at once.

"Trying to be free ain't worth it!"

"Too dangerous . . . "

"Reckon it's not worth running. Everyone gets caught!"

Suddenly, a young man named Jim, who was standing next to Harriet, spoke calmly and loudly.

"No! Everyone does not get caught. Many more escape than what ever gets told about in that newspaper. Ain't you all heard about it? About the Underground Railroad?"

A few people in the cabin nodded, but many more just stared at Jim.

"A train that goes under the ground?"

someone asked. "That they let black folks ride on?"

"Well, not exactly," Jim smiled, "but sort of. See, there are hidden paths way back in the woods and swamps that slaves follow that no one else knows about. That's what they mean by 'underground.' And along these paths every forty miles or so are houses where the runaways are fed and hidden and helped. They call these houses the 'stations.' The runaways are known as 'passengers,' and the good people who live at the stations are called the 'stationmasters.'"

"But how does anyone find the path? How do you find the right . . . um . . . station?" someone asked.

"Well, first of all . . . ," Jim began, but then he stopped quickly. Off in the distance was the sound of Master Brodas's dogs barking. Sometimes Master checked on the slaves at night, and he brought along his dogs in case of any trouble. If he found a group of slaves gathered in a cabin, all of them would be whipped. And since the Nat Turner event, slaves who were found gathering secretly were looked upon as criminals.

Harriet rushed out the door with everyone else, but not before looking back at Jim. Their eyes met for a moment. And in his eyes she saw a light that she had never seen in a slave's eyes before—it was a light of hope.

CHAPTER 3

For the next several days, Harriet tried to work near Jim out in the tobacco fields. When the overseer was too far away to hear, Jim would speak quietly about the Underground Railroad, the paths, and the slaves who had found freedom. The "overseer" was the man Master Brodas hired to watch over the slaves as they worked. And he whipped or kicked them if they did not work hard enough. He was a very fat man who seemed to particularly enjoy kicking the weaker slaves. He also thought it was funny to slap the female slaves.

"But where's that line you gotta cross to be free?" Harriet whispered to Jim one afternoon.

Jim ducked his head low and whispered back. "It's just south of Philadelphia. 'Bout 130 miles from here. Not that far."

"Not that far!?" Harriet said a little too loudly. "Seems like pretty far to walk to me."

"Ain't nothing if you want to be free," Jim whispered. "Why, there's slaves down in Carolina who have to walk three times that far. Way down there, they're glad to do anything to get free."

Just then, the overseer appeared and glared at Jim and Harriet. He spit tobacco juice in Jim's direction and said, "Y'all too quiet over here. A quiet slave means a slave who's up to no good. You better let me hear some singin', or you gonna be feelin' this whip."

Jim winked at Harriet and started singing as loudly as he could:

When that old chariot comes,
I'm going to leave you.
I'm bound for the promised land.
Friends, I'm going to leave you.
I'm bound for the promised land.

The next day, Jim was strangely silent all morning. Harriet tried to get him to talk more about the secret paths through the swamps, but he kept moving away from her and looking around. At noon, Jim stood straight up and looked out across the field toward the road. The overseer's back was turned, and he was slumped over like he was asleep.

"I reckon I need to go," Jim said in an eerily calm voice. With that, Jim began walking quickly toward the dirt road near the field. Harriet watched Jim cross the road and then break into a fast run. As if in slow motion, Harriet turned around to see the overseer rising to his feet and rubbing his eyes.

"Hey! What the . . . " The overseer suddenly came trotting past Harriet in pursuit of Jim, his fat stomach bouncing against his belt. But Jim was so far ahead that he didn't even notice the overseer following him. Quietly, Harriet followed behind the overseer. Somehow, she wanted to warn or help Jim, but she didn't know how she'd be able to do that.

Far down the dirt road, Jim's running form was barely visible, but the overseer was able to see him dodge into an old General Store.

"I got you now," the overseer muttered as he waddled as fast as he could toward the store. *Quick! Get out of the store, Jim! Run!* Harriet thought desperately as she trailed behind the overseer. But when the overseer burst through the door, Jim was standing near the front, talking quietly to a man behind the counter.

"What you think you're doing, boy? Get the hell back to that field," the overseer yelled, pulling out his whip.

In a flash, Jim was running toward the back door. At that moment, the overseer noticed

Harriet standing on the other side of the store.

"Block his way!" the overseer screamed at Harriet. "Don't let him get out that door!"

But Harriet did just the opposite. As Jim flew out the back door and into the woods, Harriet bravely stood directly in front of the overseer and spread her arms, blocking his way. His face nearly purple with rage, the overseer picked up a ten-pound weight from a scale and tried to hurl it at Jim to stop him. But the weight hit Harriet instead. She felt a tremendous blow above her left eye. Then everything went dark as she collapsed to the floor.

For nearly two hours, Harriet lay unconscious on the floor. Finally, the overseer dragged her back to her parents' cabin and threw her in the doorway. Ben and Rit rushed to their daughter's side as the overseer spit a stream of tobacco juice on the cabin floor.

"She ain't gonna live," he said with a sneer and then turned to leave.

"Wake up! Hat, wake up!" Rit and Ben sat at the breakfast table with Harriet, who had fallen asleep in the middle of eating again. Several years had passed since Harriet had been hit in the head by the weight. She had lived, but she had never been quite right since the accident. A deep dent above her left eye had damaged her brain. The damage caused her to suddenly fall asleep with no warning, often while she was eating or working.

"She ain't never gonna be normal again," Rit said with tears in her eyes as she tried to wake Harriet.

"Well, at least that means she'll stay here with us," Ben pointed out. "No one will want to buy a damaged slave."

And it was true. Master Brodas had tried to sell Harriet many times right after the accident. But with her dented head, her sleeping spells, and her stubborn refusal to even look at the possible buyers who poked and prodded her, no one was interested in paying for her. Even though an adult female slave was worth hundreds of dollars, Harriet was said to be worth less than six cents.

Even so, Harriet went back to work on the Brodas plantation. And when she found out that working fifteen or more hours a day meant that she could actually get paid a few cents a week, Harriet worked harder than ever. Harriet saved these pennies in a jar for weeks, and then months, and then a few years. She had a secret plan. Finally, when Harriet had nearly twenty dollars, she went to speak to Master Brodas.

"How much would you sell me for?" she asked, knowing that Master Brodas had not been able to sell her in the years since the been able to sell her in the years since the accident.

"What? Girl, you ain't worth six cents," Brodas said, laughing out loud at the short, strange-looking young woman. But in reality, when Brodas had realized that Harriet was as hard a worker as ever, he had decided to keep her.

"Well then, Sir, I would like to pay for my freedom with this here." Harriet proudly stuck out her jar of pennies.

Brodas looked at the jar and then at Harriet's face and realized she was serious. He doubled over laughing.

"A handful of pennies! You ignorant slave," Master Brodas barked. "Come back when you have five hundred dollars. We'll talk then." With that he slammed the door in Harriet's face, laughing meanly.

With furious tears in her eyes, Harriet slowly walked back home. *It'd take me the rest of my life to save that much money! I can't wait until I'm dead to be free.* Harriet's burning desire for freedom had never left her. And, in fact, it began burning more strongly after she had helped Jim escape. Jim had never been captured, and it was rumored that he had run all the way to New York.

And Harriet's dreams and visions had been coming to her more and more often. On many nights, Harriet would dream she was flying. Far below her were bright paths winding through dark forests and dangerous swamplands. In many of these dreams, the magical line near Philadelphia would appear below her, only to disappear before she could fly over it. And the old dream of crying, bleeding children chained together troubled her many nights. In the mornings, she would awaken knowing that God was telling her to do something. But what?

"Whoa! Hey, Harriet . . . You crying? What's wrong, baby?"

Harriet was so lost in her thoughts that she had run smack into John Tubman as she turned the corner for home. John was a young man that Harriet had been seeing for a couple months. He was a happy, talkative man who told lots of jokes to make Harriet laugh, but she didn't feel like laughing now. She explained what had happened with Master Brodas.

"Now, Hat, why you so worried about being free? You ain't gonna change the world by being free." John grinned playfully at Harriet.

"But it's wrong to be owned like some old horse or something," Harriet said. "You don't understand, John. How could you?"

Even though John was a black man living in the slave state of Maryland, he had never been a slave. His parents had paid for their freedom before he was born, so he had never known the pain and humiliation of slavery. He saw that Harriet had a place to live, work to do, and even got to keep a few pennies a week. That seemed like a good enough life to him.

"Well, I know one thing," John replied with a wink. "Soon enough, you and me gettin' married. Then I'll never be a free man again."

In spite of her sadness, Harriet had to laugh at this. John put his arm around her and leaned down to kiss the top of her head. "Stop your worryin' now. Freedom ain't everything. We got each other."

Within a year, John and Harriet were married. For a while, Harriet enjoyed her new life and all the attention John gave her, but in a fairly short time, Harriet began to see just what kind of man John really was. He was content to let Harriet work all day while he hung around the cabin sharpening his hunting knives and taking naps. Mostly, John just wanted someone to take care of him. And before long, John was no longer amused by his wife's longing for freedom.

"You're a fool, woman!" John yelled one night. "There will always be black slaves and white masters. All this nonsense about these paths and lines and white people actually helping black people along the way is crazy talk."

"No, John. The Underground Railroad

is real," Harriet said calmly. "More and more slaves are taking the Railroad. Things are changing. Why, if we could make it up to that line, then I'd be free, too, and then . . . "

John cut Harriet off abruptly. "We? WE? I ain't going on some make-believe trail through the woods. If you're ever crazy enough to do that, you're going alone. I got no interest in helping a slave run away—not even you, Harriet. I like life here just fine. Don't seem like such a bad life to me!" With that, John turned his back on Harriet and glared into the fireplace. Harriet looked at the back of her husband's head and thought, *No, I bet it doesn't seem like such a bad life to you. You're free.*

Much later that same night, a loud banging on the cabin door awoke Harriet with a start. It was her brothers Robert and Benjie.

"Hat, there's some terrible news. Master Brodas had himself a heart attack this evening and he's dead. Ain't no more Master!" Both Robert and Benjie were wringing their hands and looking as though they might cry.

Harriet looked at her brothers for a long minute. "You all come here in the middle of the night to tell me that? You expectin' me to sit down and shed even one tear over Master dyin'? More likely have a party."

"No, Hat," Robert said, shaking his head. "It ain't that. It's . . . it's . . " Harriet noticed both her brothers' hands were shaking. She grabbed Robert and Benjie and pulled them inside the cabin.

"What is it? What's wrong?"

"There's already talk that Miss Sarah gonna sell us all down South, maybe even tomorrow. Far down South to a cotton planter in Louisiana." Robert's eyes were huge as he spoke.

"Zeke says the cotton plantations is the worst," Benjie continued. "Overseers there whip slaves to death nearly every day for no reason at all."

Harriet sat down and put her head in her hands. Down South. Those were two words she had feared all her life. Now she would be hundreds and hundreds of miles further away from freedom. Life would be tremendously harder. Harriet's mind spun wildly. What to do? What to do? But then a feeling of strange calm began slowly washing over Harriet. Her head cleared, and she seemed to hear a voice speaking to her: *It's time, Harriet. It's time to go.* Harriet looked up. She had heard the words, but neither brother had said anything. And she could still hear John snoring in the other room. Suddenly, Harriet knew what to do.

"All right. Listen to me," Harriet said in a low, steady voice. "Both of you need to go and pack enough food for four days. Come back here as quick as you can. Wear strong shoes. Don't tell no one what we're doing."

Robert and Benjie looked at each other and then back at Harriet.

"But what are we doing, Hat?"

"The Underground Railroad," Harriet whispered. "We're getting on board tonight."

CHAPTER 4

As soon as Robert and Benjie left to gather their supplies, Harriet grabbed a large leather sack that John used when he went hunting. Into this sack she quickly and quietly loaded most of the food she could find, taking great care not to wake up John in the process. *If he wakes and sees what I'm doing, won't be no chance of escape tonight,* Harriet thought.

After packing the little money she had and the only other set of clothes she owned, Harriet looked around their tiny cabin. In one corner were John's hunting knives. Carefully, Harriet took the longest and sharpest knife and placed it in the sack. In the other corner of the cabin sat a new pair of work boots that John had recently bought with some of Harriet's money. *Don't know why a man who never works needs work boots,* Harriet considered. Then she slipped on John's boots and tiptoed outside to meet her brothers.

"Hat, looks like a bad storm comin' our way," Benjie whispered nervously as the three began walking quickly down the road and toward the dark woods that Harriet had watched Jim escape to years ago.

"A little rain ain't gonna hurt us," Harriet whispered back. But a terrible late-summer storm was moving in quickly with dangerous lightning and a drenching downpour. Soaked to the skin within minutes, Harriet and her two brothers began groping along a faint trail in the woods.

"How we gonna know if we're going the right way?" Robert asked, with the clear sound of fear in his voice. "Can't see no North Star tonight. Hat, how you know we're not headed further south?"

Just then a huge flash of lightning lit up the woods. Harriet's brothers watched as she leaned over close to the base of an old oak tree, calmly feeling around it with her hands.

"We're headed the right way," Harriet snapped, irritated that her brothers were so quick to be doubtful and afraid. "Jim done taught me that moss only grows on the north side of tree trunks. That's the way we're going. Now hush. We got a long ways to go tonight."

But soon, the faint trail disappeared altogether. From her talks with Jim, Harriet knew that if they just continued north along the Choptank River, they would reach another road in about nine miles. And this road would lead to another trail. But Robert and Benjie began to panic.

"I don't know about this, Hat. We could get lost," Benjie complained. "Those slave catchers will be out after us first thing tomorrow, and if we don't even know where we are . . . "

"Benjie's right," Robert agreed quickly, his voice shaking as the thunder boomed. "Maybe we should head back and plan this a little better and leave again in a few days or so. This is too dangerous tonight."

Harriet stopped and turned to face her brothers. As the lightning flashed, they could clearly see a fire in her eyes.

"Ain't ever gonna be a night that isn't dangerous for running away," Harriet said slowly and clearly. "I have faith that God will protect us all the way to that line. But if y'all are too afraid, then go home now before we get any further."

There was a long moment of silence as Robert and Benjie were reluctant to meet their sister's eyes again.

"But what about you, Hat?" Benjie finally asked.

"Me? I intend to ride this train to the end. Ain't no turning back for me," Harriet answered confidently.

Some minutes later, after tearful hugs and useless pleading with Harriet to return with them, Robert and Benjie said goodbye to their sister. In the flashes of lightning, the brothers watched the strange sight of a young woman barely five feet tall walking away in too-big boots with a huge leather sack tossed across her back.

"I know one thing," Robert said as he and Benjie watched Harriet disappear into the stormy night alone. "That woman is braver than any man I've ever known."

Hours later, Harriet sloshed out of a swampy field and onto the road that would lead to the next trail. Exhausted and covered with weeds and mud, Harriet headed up the road straining her eyes in the dark for an old abandoned barn that marked the beginning of the trail. Though it had been years ago, Harriet had never forgotten the directions Jim had given her. However, his directions went no further than this second trail. It would, supposedly, lead her another twenty miles to the home of an Underground Railroad "stationmaster," Mr. Ezekiel Hunn. He would give her the next set of directions.

Mr. Hunn and his wife, Jim had explained,

were Quakers—kind, soft-spoken people who hated slavery and were glad to help runaways. There were plenty of white people in the South who hated slavery, but they were often afraid to help runaway slaves. Many of the Quakers, however, were willing to take the risk.

"You can trust a Quaker 'bout as much as you can trust a black man," Jim had always said. "Sometimes more."

Morning sunlight was just beginning to creep through the trees when Harriet spotted the barn up ahead. This was a great relief since it would be exceedingly dangerous for her to walk along the road in broad daylight. Slave catchers would be out with their dogs, rifles, and whips as soon as the sun was up.

As tired as she was, Harriet knew there was no time to sleep—not until she was at least ten miles or more into the next trail. She was still too close to the Brodas plantation, and word of her escape might already be out. Even so, when Harriet reached the old barn, she decided to hide behind it for just a few minutes in order to have a bite of soggy cornbread. But as Harriet began eating, a familiar old feeling began to settle over her quickly, a feeling she could neither stop nor control . . .

"I'd rather just shoot any of these filthy runaways than take the trouble to drag 'em back alive."

"Or whip 'em 'til they can't see straight and then shoot 'em!"

Harriet awoke with a jump. One of her sleeping spells had come over her while she had been eating. She didn't know how long she had been asleep, but the sun was high overhead, and loud, crude voices were booming from the other side of the barn. With her heart hammering and her hand gripping the big knife she had packed, Harriet peeked around the barn. Slave catchers! Four white men armed with rifles and whips were slowly passing by on horses. Harriet barely breathed as she waited for them to disappear down the road. As soon as they were out of sight, Harriet ran to the faint path and didn't stop running until the barn and the road were far behind her.

All afternoon and late into the night, Harriet continued to walk. Tonight, the North Star was shining brightly, and it seemed to be calling to her to hurry. Once, she thought she heard the howling of tracking dogs, and she broke into a run again. She had heard some terrible stories about how these dogs were trained to attack runaways and pin them down. An unfortunate runaway who struggled against the dogs could have his flesh ripped from his bones by the dogs' sharp teeth. Harriet found a creek alongside the path and walked in it knee deep for nearly a mile. The dogs would not be able to follow her scent now.

Finally, as the morning sun was rising higher, Harriet came to a cornfield where the path suddenly ended. Just to the right of the cornfield was a white farmhouse surrounded by sunflowers and rosebushes. Could this be Ezekiel Hunn's house? Harriet hid behind a tree and watched the house for nearly an hour. Finally a young white woman came out to the front porch with a broom. She was dressed in the simple grey dress of the Quakers. This must be the right place, Harriet thought nervously to herself. But Harriet was fearful of approaching a white person to ask for help. *What if I'm wrong? What if . . . ?* Harriet hid behind the tree until she grew angry with herself. *You fool! Stop worrying! God has guided you here. You can't hide behind this tree forever.*

"Pardon me, Missus," Harriet said shyly and politely as she approached the young woman, afraid to look directly at her. "Does a Master Hunn live here?"

The woman stared at Harriet for a moment and then did something that terrified Harriet.

"Here," the woman said in a low voice as she handed Harriet the broom. "Start sweeping." Then the woman went back inside her house.

Oh no! Harriet's mind spun wildly. *She*

thinks I'm one of her slaves. I've come to the wrong house!

At that moment, a young man also dressed in the plain clothes of the Quakers walked out the front door. With him was another man who carried a rifle and was definitely not a Quaker. Harriet kept her head low and continued sweeping.

"Well then, you be careful, Mr. Hunn," the man with the rifle said as he got on his horse. "Them runaways can be dangerous."

"Yes sir, I certainly will keep an eye out for runaways. Thank you so much for letting me know that some may be in this area," the Quaker man said with a broad grin. He watched the man with the rifle ride away. Then he turned to Harriet and reached out his hand for hers.

"I'm Ezekiel Hunn," he said warmly, grasping Harriet's hand. "My wife and I apologize for our strange behavior, but we wanted that man to think you worked for us. You do understand and accept our apology, I hope." Ezekiel bowed slightly as he spoke.

Harriet was stunned. A white person had rarely ever spoken kindly to her. Certainly no white person had ever apologized to her for anything.

"Why . . . yes, Master Hunn . . . I . . . " Harriet began.

"Call me Ezekiel. There is no 'master' here," Ezekiel said with a kind smile. "And who might you be?"

"Harriet. Harriet Tubman. I was told that you might be able to help me."

"Yes, Harriet. You've found a station on the Railroad. And I can tell you how to reach your next stop. But first, how about breakfast?"

For the next few days, Harriet rested and ate. It was the first time she had ever slept in a real bed with sheets and pillows or eaten such unusual foods as roasted lamb or chocolate pie. Mrs. Hunn washed and mended Harriet's clothes while Ezekiel told Harriet what she must do next to get to the line of freedom.

"I have sent word ahead to the next station about you. Tomorrow evening, I will drive you in my wagon for the next forty miles," Ezekiel explained. "Then you will follow a long trail that leads to a graveyard. You must hide in the graveyard and wait for a ticket for the next part of your journey."

Ticket? Harriet wondered. *What kind of tickets they handing out in graveyards?* But Harriet would find out soon enough.

The next night, Harriet crawled out of the back of Ezekiel's old wagon, where she had been hidden beneath flour sacks. Ezekiel pointed to the path. "Move quickly now, Harriet," he whispered. "The further north you get, the more slave catchers there will be looking for you. There's likely notices posted about your escape by now."

Harriet thanked Ezekiel and hurried down the faint path. She had fifteen miles to walk, and it would take her the rest of the night. Ezekiel's words had frightened Harriet, and with every little sound and snap of a twig, Harriet reached into her sack and grabbed the big knife. *No slave catchers will take me back alive,* Harriet thought fiercely. *I will fight for my liberty, and if the time comes for me to go, the Lord will let them kill me.*

Just before dawn, Harriet found herself in a small graveyard. Exhausted, she sat down behind a huge tombstone and waited for her "ticket" to arrive. Within minutes, she heard heavy footsteps approaching her quickly. Harriet jumped up and whirled around with the knife in her hand.

"Careful . . . careful. I am a friend. I've brought you your ticket." A young black man dressed in work clothes handed Harriet some clothes, a hat, and a shovel.

"What?" Harriet asked, confused. "This is my . . . ticket? I don't understand."

"You gotta change your clothes quickly and dress as a man," he explained. "This morning we gonna cross the bridge into Delaware. It is the only way across, and it is closely guarded by many slave catchers. No one will look twice at two black men walking to work. But they'd be on you—a black woman traveling alone—before you'd get your toe on that bridge."

Without another word, Harriet quickly disguised herself as a workingman. Within thirty minutes, she and the young man were walking across the bridge into Delaware, carrying shovels. Harriet was sure that her pounding heart would give her away. At either end of the bridge were white men holding rifles and glaring at the black passersby, but they didn't seem particularly interested in two black men going to work on a Thursday morning.

Once on the other side of the bridge, the young man led Harriet down a quiet street and pointed to a small, neat house.

"There's your next station," he whispered. "Thomas Garrett is the stationmaster, and he's expecting you." With that, the young man grasped Harriet's hand and stared at her for a moment. Then he pulled off his hat as a sign of respect.

"You gonna make it, Miz Tubman," he whispered. "Ain't got far to go now."

CHAPTER 5

"Quickly, quickly!" A white man with gray hair and a kind but worried face pulled Harriet into his house and shut the door in a hurry.

"We must be extremely careful," Thomas Garrett explained in a half-whisper, even though Harriet was now behind closed doors in a dark room with all the curtains pulled tight. Thomas tiptoed to the window, pulled the curtains aside just a sliver, and stared out into the street for several seconds. Then he turned back to Harriet.

"Follow me," he said, taking her hand and leading her up a long staircase. Just before they reached the top, Thomas stopped at a bookcase. Pushing the bookcase aside, a small secret door was revealed. He opened the door and led Harriet into a tiny windowless room with a bed, a table, and two oil lamps. Thomas Garrett lit a lamp and finally looked relaxed.

"Now," he said with a relieved smile, "So pleased to meet you, Harriet. I'm Thomas Garrett. I hope you will be comfortable in this room for the next few days."

"Yes sir, Master . . . uh . . . Mister Garrett," Harriet said quietly. "But . . . why do I have to wait three days? Isn't this the last station? You ain't sending another message ahead to anyone, are you?"

"No, Harriet," Thomas said, shaking his head slowly. "But we must wait until Sunday morning, when all the slave catchers are in church. I will take you in my carriage to a spot that is only a few miles from the Pennsylvania border."

"You mean the line, Mr. Garrett?" Harriet said almost in a whisper.

Thomas Garrett smiled knowingly. He had been hiding and helping runaway slaves for several years, and he had seen the same look of excitement and awe on many slaves' faces.

"Yes, Harriet—the line."

As exhausted as she was from her journey, Harriet found it difficult to sleep the next few nights. Freedom! The word rolled over and over again in her head, beating like a drum. Finally, Sunday morning arrived, and she and Thomas

Garrett were gone in his carriage before sunrise. Thomas disguised Harriet in a heavy black shawl and veil that hid her face—anyone seeing them would assume that Thomas's passenger was a white woman. After a couple hours of quick riding, Thomas stopped and pointed into the woods.

"You will find a very clear path just beyond these trees. Follow it for about an hour and you will see a signpost." Here, Thomas paused to smile at Harriet, his eyes twinkling. "Step past the sign, and you will be free."

Harriet thanked Thomas Garrett many times over and then disappeared into the woods and onto the well-worn path. She was so excited that she began quietly singing:

I'll meet you in the morning
When you reach the promised land;
On the other side of the Jordan
For I'm bound for the promised land!

Suddenly, the signpost appeared. Tears filled Harriet's eyes as she stepped slowly across the line. Many years later, she described how she felt when she crossed the state line: "I looked at my hands to see if I was the same person now I was free. There was such a glory over everything. The sun came like gold through the trees and over the fields, and I felt like I was in heaven."

Harriet followed the road that led to Philadelphia all day. There was no longer any need to hide on secret trails or to wear disguises—she was as free as the white people hurrying by in fancy carriages. Harriet was so thrilled that she smiled and waved to everyone who passed. But something was wrong. In her dreams, she had seen beautiful white women reaching out to her to help and comfort her once she entered the land of freedom. But no one returned her smiles or welcomed her. In fact, many people frowned and turned away when she waved at them.

I'm free, but there's no one here to welcome me to the land of freedom, Harriet thought. I'm just a stranger in a strange land! Harriet continued down the busy yet lonely road until the tall steeples and buildings of Philadelphia finally came into view in the evening sun. Having never seen a big city before, Harriet was stunned. She could hardly believe that so many buildings and roads and carriages and roaring trains and rushing people could all be in one place. As she cautiously walked into the city, everyone and everything seemed to be speeding by her. With no place to go and no one to help her, Harriet sat down on a curb and watched the busy city for most of the night. Near dawn, Harriet wondered, *Will I ever find my way in this strange land?*

●　　●　　●

The very next day, Harriet did indeed begin finding her way. Fearless, smart, and no stranger to hard work, Harriet figured that if she could just find some big, fancy homes, there would be plenty of work for her to do. And she was right. After knocking on only a few doors, Harriet was in business.

"Would you scrub floors and wash windows?" a tall woman asked.

"Yes ma'am," Harriet answered, astonished at being asked if she would do work instead of being told that she must do it.

"Well, then," the tall lady continued, "I have a week's worth of cleaning for you to do. I can pay you three dollars, but you won't get it until the job is finished."

"Yes ma'am," was all Harriet could manage to say. Three dollars! After years of only earning a few cents a week now and then, this seemed an unimaginable amount of money.

That evening, Harriet found a clean and inexpensive room to rent. At the end of the week, she collected her three dollars and began knocking on other doors, looking for other jobs. In this way, Harriet worked many different kinds of jobs, enjoying the freedom to decide how her days would go and how she would live her life. In particular, Harriet loved using her spare time to explore all the wonders of Philadelphia. Down every street she walked were people of all different colors, working together and living side by side. There were no masters or overseers with whips. Exotic and delicious smells drifted out of restaurants. Harriet discovered ice cream one night and street musicians the next. It seemed to Harriet that there was no end to the treasures of the city.

One Sunday afternoon, Harriet was sitting under a shade tree across the street from a large red brick building. It looked something like a church, but many people kept walking in and out of it. She noticed more than a few black people walking in and then coming back out smiling and talking excitedly. Finally, Harriet crossed the street and entered the building. Above the doorway was the name of the building, but Harriet was unable to read it.

Once inside, Harriet saw a small group of people gathered around a big bell, silently looking at it. Harriet moved in for a closer look. *I don't understand this,* she thought. *It's just an old bell with a crack in it!* But then Harriet noticed a young black girl, about twelve years old, who was walking around the bell, looking at it closely, and speaking quietly to herself. *She's reading something,* Harriet thought. Harriet moved next to the girl.

"What's that you're reading?" Harriet asked quietly.

The girl looked up at Harriet and smiled in a friendly way. "It's the Liberty Bell. Come here," she said, grabbing Harriet's hand. "We have to start at the beginning. The words go around the bell."

Harriet stared at the bell as the young girl slowly read: "Proclaim Liberty throughout all the land and unto all the inhabitants thereof."

Harriet was quiet for a long moment and then said, "So, that bell's saying that everyone in this land ought to be free?"

The young girl's mother who was standing behind Harriet put her hand on Harriet's shoulder and said, "That's right. Gonna come a day, and it won't be long, when there won't be any such thing as a slave. You wait and see."

That night, Harriet tossed and turned. Something had been bothering her ever since she had arrived in Philadelphia, and now the words on the Liberty Bell had made everything crystal clear to her. *Liberty throughout ALL the land,* Harriet thought. *I'm still a stranger in a strange land because my family still isn't free!* Harriet thought long and hard about her brothers, sister, and her parents who were still bound in the chains of slavery. Beyond that, there were three million more slaves in the United States. As Harriet finally drifted off to sleep, her old horrible visions of crying and bleeding slave children all chained together pounded through her head. The next morning when she awoke, Harriet knew what she must do.

"The silver one with the black handle." Harriet was in a small shop in Philadelphia buying a gun. Six months had passed since she had seen the Liberty Bell—six months of saving money and making plans. Tomorrow she would be heading back down to Maryland to gather her sister and her sister's family. Being a "conductor" on the Underground Railroad was much more dangerous than being a runaway, so Harriet wanted to be prepared.

On her way out of town the next morning, Harriet stopped by the house of a friend, William Still. William was a free black man who worked for the Pennsylvania Anti-Slavery Society. Harriet had met him at a meeting she had wandered into some months earlier, and William had instantly been struck by Harriet's stories and her fearlessness. But this morning William was afraid for his friend Harriet.

"I wish you would change your mind, Harriet. If you get caught doing this . . . "

"Won't get caught," Harriet interrupted. "God will keep me safe."

"But Harriet," William Still continued, "a woman should not be a conductor. It's never been done. A man is better suited to the job."

Harriet knew her friend was concerned about her, but suddenly she was angry. "Now look here. I done worked as hard as any man for twenty-four years. I made my way to freedom on my own, and now I intend to help my family. I'm not afraid of what I have to do, and I sure ain't afraid just because I'm a woman!"

William Still looked at Harriet, shook his head, and smiled. He knew that her heart was set and that fear was not an option. "Well then, Harriet. I will see you when you return. Godspeed, my friend."

Harriet's trip back to Maryland was quick and safe. Slave catchers were not looking for black people headed south. However, the trip back up to Philadelphia was not as easy. Harriet's sister and brother-in-law had two small children who were not able to travel as quickly or endure many of the hardships Harriet had endured during her escape. Even so, Harriet prayed daily and kept her eyes on the North Star nightly. Within ten days, she had returned to Philadelphia with her sister's family.

Encouraged by her success, Harriet returned to Maryland several weeks later to guide her oldest brother and two of his friends to freedom. And although they had to outrun an overseer, hide in bat-filled caves, and wade through icy rivers in order to lose tracking dogs, the group also arrived safely in Philadelphia.

Finally, after much thought, Harriet decided to return to Maryland once again—this time to ask John Tubman to come to Philadelphia so that they could continue as husband and wife. After all, they were married, and in spite of their arguments, Harriet still loved John and missed him. She still longed to raise a family with him. So on a warm spring evening after a quick journey back to Maryland and the old Brodas plantation, Harriet found herself knocking on the old cabin door. There was no answer, so Harriet knocked again.

"Who you looking for?" A young female slave that Harriet didn't recognize finally answered the door.

"John Tubman . . . my husband," Harriet replied.

The young slave gave Harriet a funny look. "Reckon he ain't your husband anymore," she said. "He's left 'bout a year ago with his new wife, Caroline. She a slave on the Jackson plantation."

Harriet stared at the woman. "Married? But . . . he's . . . he's . . . "

"He's gone is what he is. Said you done run off and left him first." With that, the young woman just shook her head and shut the door of what used to be Harriet and John's cabin.

Harriet tried to fight back her tears as she walked quietly through the rows of cabins. But as quickly as the tears had come, they were gone. As though a clear voice had spoken to her again, Harriet suddenly understood that her life's focus would not be her husband or a family of her own. God had a different path for her; she must continue to guide her people to freedom. Like Moses of old, Harriet would lead the slaves out of bondage. This would be her life's mission.

So, tiptoeing to windows and tapping on doors, Harriet whispered that the train to freedom would be leaving that night. Did anyone want to get on board? Yes! Again and again, the excited answers came back. Yes! By the time the moon was high, a large group had gathered at the dark end of the fields by the road. Harriet softly sang, *When that old chariot comes, who's going with me?* as she led the slaves across the road, into the woods, along the old path, and north to freedom.

Five days later, William Still sat in his office with a troubled expression on his face. In his hands, he held a poster that had been sent to him by his friend Thomas Garrett. Thomas had written that dozens of these posters were up all through Delaware and Maryland. Near the top of the poster was a drawing of a young black woman with a scowl on her face and a dent above her left eye. Below the picture, in large, bold letters, William read:

Wanted:
Harriet Tubman
For Escape and for
Aiding in the Escape of Others

Reward of $15,000.00
Wanted Dead or Alive!

CHAPTER 6

Three days later, Harriet sat in William Still's office with a little smile on her face as she stared at the poster.

"Harriet, I can't imagine why in the world you would be smiling about this," William said. "This is quite serious."

"Well, first of all, that picture sure don't look like me," Harriet said, still grinning.

William rubbed his neck and shook his head. "That doesn't matter! Don't you understand? You are the only woman leading slaves to freedom. It will be very easy for the slave catchers to spot you—this is exactly what I warned you about. Harriet, your life is in danger!"

Harriet stopped smiling and looked at her friend. "They won't ever catch me. I know in my soul that they won't. Never!"

A long silence filled William's office. Then, slowly, a big grin crossed Harriet's face again. "And second of all," Harriet continued, "You say that poster reads that there's a $15,000.00 reward for me?"

William nodded.

"Well, then, I sure come a long ways from the day I wasn't even worth six cents."

All that next year, Harriet continued to travel back to Maryland and Virginia and bring groups of slaves up to freedom. The higher the reward for her capture became, the more dangerous her trips became. Slave catchers began focusing on tracking down this Harriet Tubman who was becoming known as "Moses" to the slaves throughout the South.

So to protect herself, Harriet became a master of disguises. Often, she dressed as a very old woman. She would carry a cane and hunch over, an old bonnet on her head and a shawl on her shoulders. She was even able to mimic the voice of an old woman. Disguised in this way, Harriet could travel south on trains to meet up with slaves and then guide them northward by the old trails. Not having to walk the 180 miles south to meet up with her groups was worth the few dollars it cost to ride the train. No one ever looked twice at an elderly black woman headed south—until one afternoon.

Harriet's sleeping spells had never gone away completely, and one day while waiting to change trains in Delaware, she suddenly fell asleep. Although she was disguised, this was still exceedingly dangerous. When Harriet finally awoke with a start, two men sitting across from her in the station were both staring closely at her and talking quietly. Harriet kept her eyes closed so that the men would think she was still asleep.

"I'm telling you that I think that's her," said the first man.

"No, she's too old. Look," whispered the other, pointing to something above Harriet's head. "That says that this Tubman woman is young and very strong. This couldn't be the right person."

The first man stared for a moment just above Harriet's head and said, "Well, for a reward of $15,000.00, I say we just grab this old woman and make sure."

Harriet froze. Because she couldn't read, she had sat down directly below a "wanted" poster for her own capture! Thinking quickly, Harriet acted as though she had just awakened. Then, adjusting her fake granny glasses, she reached for a newspaper someone had left beside her and began to pretend that she was reading it. I hope I don't have this paper upside-down, Harriet thought desperately. The first man stared a moment longer at Harriet and then looked disappointed.

"Come on," he said, standing up. "You're right. That must not be her. All these posters say that the Tubman woman can't read or write."

Harriet sighed a long sigh of relief and stuffed the newspaper into her bag to use another time.

Over the course of a couple years and many trips to help free her people, Harriet became an expert conductor. She also started to become something of a legend among slaves all through the South. Whisperings, rumors, and stories began spreading like wildfire:

"They say Moses can disappear into thin air, and she can fly when she needs to."

"She's strong enough to pull trees from the ground to make the path clearer and wider."

"Heard she's got her a gun and she'll use it if she has to."

Many of the stories were simply exaggerations of the excitement that thousands of slaves felt when they learned about this amazing woman who kept the slave catchers running in circles and looking like fools. However, it was no exaggeration about her gun.

Once, on a particularly cold and hard trip up north, a young male slave became exhausted and frightened. His feet were blistered and painful, and in the distance, the slave catchers' rifle shots and tracking dogs could be heard.

"Miss Harriet, I'm just gonna stop here and head back home. Guess I ain't strong enough to make it," the young man said in a shaky voice.

Harriet sat down next to him and patiently explained that he could not turn around. "No turning back now, son," she said as she helped bandage his bloody feet and gave him some of her own food.

"But I can't do it. I just can't," the man argued.

Harriet lowered her voice so the rest of the group would not be alarmed. "Now listen to me. I don't care how much you're hurting or scared—you are not turning back. You go back and your old master will beat and torture the truth out of you. I can't risk everyone's lives in this group just because your feet are hurting!"

Then the young man got angry and stood up. "You ain't gonna tell me what I can and can't do. Ain't gonna have a woman boss me around," he yelled. "I believe I'll be leaving right now." He turned to walk back on the trail when he suddenly felt something cold and hard on the back of his head.

"I believe you won't," came Harriet's steely voice. The young man whirled around to see a silver pistol with a black handle pointed directly at his head.

"You wouldn't . . . " the young man began.

"I would," came Harriet's calm reply. "Dead slaves can't tell no stories. You go on with the rest of us or die. You choose."

With that, the young man joined the group and never complained with even one word for the rest of the journey. And though Harriet never had to shoot a slave that wanted to turn back, she always swore that she would have if she had had to. "If he was weak enough to give up," she explained, "he'd be weak enough to betray us all."

Harriet still had three brothers, Benjie, Robert, and Henry, who had not yet escaped to freedom. Since they were Harriet's brothers, they were closely watched—even guarded. One day, their new master decided that they were too much of a risk to keep on his plantation, so he made plans to sell all three brothers to a rice grower way down in Mississippi.

"Should've gone with Hat when she tried to lead us to freedom three years ago," Benjie said bitterly. "Now we got no chance. Gonna be slaves 'til we die."

"But there must be some way we can get a message to her," Henry said thoughtfully.

"Every black person from here to Philadelphia knows who our sister is by now. We can ask for a message to be passed along."

In less than a week, Harriet got the news. All three of her brothers would be allowed to spend Christmas Day with their parents, Ben and Rit. But the next day, they would be on their way for good to a big rice plantation near the Gulf of Mexico.

No time to spare! Harriet thought with a worried frown. It was already Christmas Eve. Quickly, Harriet packed her bag, dressed in disguise as a man, and ran to catch the next train down to Maryland. By that evening, Harriet was moving quietly and very quickly along the snowy trail that led to Ben and Rit's. She prayed that she would catch her brothers before they reached their parents' house. About a half mile before she reached the house, Harriet saw three shadowy figures ahead of her.

"Benjie!" Harriet called quietly to her youngest and favorite brother. All three brothers jumped and turned around.

"Hat? Hat, is that you?" Robert asked, straining his eyes in the dark.

"I can't believe it!" Benjie shouted as he ran toward his sister. "Just in time! Now we can all spend Christmas with Ma and Daddy before you lead us out of here."

Harriet hugged her brothers tightly, but then she shook her head. "No. We can't see Ma and Daddy tonight. We'll sleep in the barn next to their house and leave at the crack of dawn before they wake up."

Harriet's brothers stared at her as though she had lost her mind. "What?" Henry asked. "Why on earth would we do that? They're expecting us tonight."

Harriet fought back tears as she spoke. "I ain't seen Ma or Daddy in years, and there's nothing I'd like better than to sit around the fire with them tonight. But it's too dangerous."

"Dangerous?" Benjie asked. "But Hat, why? No one knows you're here."

"And I aim to keep it that way," Harriet said firmly. "Benjie, when it's been discovered that all three of you are gone, the first place those slave catchers is gonna run to is Ma and Daddy's cabin. And you all know as well as me that Ma never could tell a lie. She just can't."

Harriet's brothers sighed. They knew she was right. Ma would tell the truth—and the hunt for all of them would triple in intensity if the slave catchers knew Harriet was involved. Plus, there was a good chance that Ben and Rit would be badly punished. It was too dangerous. So the four of them huddled together that Christmas Eve in the small barn across from Ben and Rit's cabin.

Through cracks in the barn's thin walls, Harriet could see her mother walk out to the front porch again and again to peer down the snowy path for her sons. Each time, she would sadly shake her head and return to the fire inside. Finally, around midnight, Rit came out to look one last time. Then, through the small window in the cabin, Harriet watched her mother sit down by the fire, put her head in her hands, and cry. *Ain't nothing ever hurt like this,* Harriet thought as she cried herself to sleep. *But it'll all be worth it, Ma. I'm coming back soon as I can to take you and Daddy to freedom, too.*

The trip back to Philadelphia with her brothers was bitterly cold, and a terrible snowstorm blew icy winds at their backs and through their thin coats the whole way. The snow and ice on the trails ripped at Harriet's worn out shoes until she literally walked her shoes off her feet. By the time Harriet found places for her brothers to stay in Philadelphia and then walked home, she had such a high fever that even the cold winter air felt hot. Harriet collapsed on the floor of her small rented room—unconscious and close to death.

"It's okay, Harriet. Everything's all right."

Harriet awoke three days later to find her friend, William Still, at her side. She had a pounding headache and very sore feet.

"But I must get up and . . . " Harriet began. William immediately blocked Harriet's ability to sit up.

"Oh no you don't. You are lucky to be alive, Harriet. The doctor says you will need to rest for at least a few weeks."

"A few weeks! Ain't got time to be laying around a few weeks," Harriet said in a hoarse voice.

"You don't have a choice, Harriet. The doctor says that . . . " William went off into a long description of what the doctor had said, but Harriet wasn't listening. What was that noise outside her window? Many voices seemed to be chanting something over and over again. Other voices were yelling and screaming. Harriet strained to hear. Let them go! Let them go! Harriet felt a cold chill run down her back. Let who go? she wondered with a strange dread.

Before William could stop her, Harriet jumped out of her bed and staggered to her window. Down below in the street, a terrible sight met her eyes. Four black men, two black women and three children were all chained together. They were being led through the streets by grinning slave catchers who carried long whips. The black men's backs were bright red with blood from whippings. On either side, crowds of angry white people screamed for their release.

Harriet spun around to face William. "What . . . what is this?" She asked, her voice shaking with anger and fear.

William turned away quickly so that Harriet wouldn't see the tears in his eyes. Then he slammed his fist against the wall. Finally, he turned back around to answer Harriet.

"I wish I didn't have to tell you this," William began. "But two days ago a new law was passed called 'The Fugitive Slave Law.'"

"'Fugitive.'" Harriet repeated. "That means runaways." William nodded and continued.

"The new law says that runaways can be captured anywhere in the United States now and returned to their masters as their master's property. What's worse, a master doesn't even have to provide proof—if he claims a black person is his slave, that person can be chained and sent back south. And what with the high-dollar capture rewards, plenty of people even in the northern states are looking to capture runaways."

Harriet stared at William, dumbfounded. "But that means . . . " she said nearly in a whisper, "That means no black person is truly safe anymore."

"Not in this country, anyway," William said

angrily. "I'm afraid the new line of freedom just moved 300 miles north to the Canadian border."

Without a word, Harriet limped over to her old beaten up bag and began stuffing belongings in it again.

"Harriet, you can't be serious. You are far too sick to travel yet. Another trip like the last one could be the death of you," William protested.

Harriet turned to face her friend, the old fire suddenly strong in her eyes. "There are two things I've got a right to, and these are death or liberty. One or the other, I mean to have."

CHAPTER 7

Harriet lay in a coffin in the back of an old hearse carriage as it moved slowly through Buffalo, New York. On either side of her were two more coffins. In them lay an escaped slave and his wife. In the woman's arms lay a young slave child. The hearse continued to the edge of town, and then it picked up speed as it raced north. Finally, it came to an abrupt stop. The driver of the hearse, a white man in a dark suit, came around back and opened the door.

"All clear," he said in a low voice. Slowly, the top of Harriet's coffin creaked open.

"What a ride!" Harriet said as she sat up and blinked her eyes. Then she tapped on the lids of the other two coffins. Immediately, they popped open, and the family of three looked around nervously.

"Are we there?" the young mother

whispered as she held her daughter close to her.

"Just about," Harriet said, climbing out of her coffin with a stretch and grabbing her travel sack. "We've got to cross the bridge over Niagara Falls first. Then y'all will be free."

The booming thunder of the falls nearly drowned out Harriet's thanks to their undertaker driver who had hidden them in his hearse. The undertaker just smiled and said, "These strange times call for strange escapes!"

And it was true. In the six months since the Fugitive Slave Law had gone into effect, hundreds of black people had fled to Canada. Thousands of white people were very angry about the new law that put their black friends in danger once again. As a result, new and unusual escape help poured in from strangers: hidden compartments in wagons, wilder disguises, and even rides in coffins.

Harriet had taken no time to rest. Though sick and limping, Harriet had continued to pray the same prayer she first spoke as an eight-year-old: God, make me strong and able to fight. And in short time, Harriet had made a daring and dangerous return trip south to rescue her parents. Fighting the cold and dodging the increased number of slave catchers who were hunting for "Moses," Harriet hid her parents in the back of a borrowed hay wagon. She then drove the wagon so fast that it often took corners on two wheels. Before the trip was half over, the horse that pulled the wagon was near death from exhaustion and had to be replaced.

Harriet settled her parents, and then her brothers, in the small town of St. Catharine's in Ontario, Canada. It was just across the border, not far from the roar of Niagara Falls. Hundreds of escaped slaves and black people who simply no longer felt safe in the United States came to St. Catharine's to start life over again. Ben and Rit were thrilled to be free after a lifetime of slavery, though they wished Harriet would settle down in St. Catharine's too, and no longer risk her life.

"Hat, you done plenty," Rit pleaded as Harriet packed to leave again. "Stay here with us, now. Why, you brought more than 100 people over that line and to Philadelphia. Time now for you to rest."

"Ma, don't you understand?" Harriet asked. "I can't trust Uncle Sam with my people no longer. They're not safe anymore until they get to Canada. When I get the message that someone needs my help, I have to go."

One "message" that particularly upset Harriet involved a young slave named Joe Bailey. Joe was strong, hardworking, and obedient to his master, but one day, something happened that changed Joe forever.

"Get on over here, boy, and take your shirt off," Joe's master demanded. The master was holding a bullwhip, the horrible whip usually used only on slaves that had committed the worst "crimes."

"But, Master, what'd I do? I ain't done nothing wrong!" Joe's eyes were wide with fear and confusion.

The master laughed and said, "I know that, boy. You're about as good a slave as you can be. I got no troubles with you. I just want to make sure you remember who's in charge around here. Give you a good beating, and you won't ever forget."

With that, Joe's master whipped Joe brutally, leaving him to crawl back home on his own. That night, Joe lay awake for hours. He had heard plenty about the woman all the slaves called "Moses." *I will NEVER allow anyone to whip me again,* Joe thought angrily. *Somehow, I'm gonna get a message to Moses. She'll lead me to freedom.* Within two weeks, Joe heard a low singing outside his cabin window late one night:

Good news, the chariot's coming,
Good news, the chariot's coming,
Good news, the chariot's coming,
An' I don't want it to leave me behind.

• • •

Moses! Joe leapt out of bed and grabbed his belongings quickly. Soon he was on the trail with Harriet and four other slaves, and Joe's heart was soaring with happiness. But the happiness didn't last long. Almost immediately, Harriet and her group heard the dogs and guns of slave catchers. The group ran all night. Harriet sprinkled spices on the trail to throw the dogs off. But at one point, the group saw the lanterns of different slave catchers just ahead of them on a trail, heading in their direction. Harriet and her group had no choice but to stand chin-deep in freezing water as the men with rifles passed by them only ten feet away.

The next days were no better. The group was split up so that they could be hidden under floorboards in different safe Quaker homes. Finally meeting back up again after hiding in mice-infested holes for days, the group was forced to take the long way up to New York to avoid capture. To make matters worse, Joe was terrified to see posters everywhere for his capture. At first, the reward had been for $500, but as the group got closer to freedom, the price for Joe shot up to $1500. And Joe was shocked to see that the price for a "dead or alive" capture of Harriet had reached $40,000.

When the group finally crossed into New

York, Joe nervously asked Harriet how many more miles were left.

"Not far, Joe," Harriet smiled. "Only about 100 miles and then we'll take a train across the bridge over Niagara Falls. You'll be free after that!"

A hundred miles! Joe put his head in his hands. From that point on, Joe did not smile. He spoke to no one and barely ate. He was so certain that they would all be captured that his spirit had given up, and he lost faith in this woman he knew as Moses. But finally the day came when the group boarded the train that would cross the bridge stretching over Niagara Falls.

"Joe! You're almost there," Harriet said brightly as they boarded the train. "Be sure to look at the Falls." But Joe kept his head down, fearing the worst. The other slaves sang excitedly and stared down at the magnificent thundering falls beneath them.

"Joe, come and look at the Falls!" Still, Joe sat sadly with his head in his hands.

"For heaven's sake, Joe, look down at the Falls, you fool, It's your last chance!" Harriet shouted across the aisle. But Joe remained still as stone.

When the train came to a stop, safe in Canada, Harriet quietly came over to Joe and took his hand. "You're free, Joe."

Slowly, as though coming out of a deep sleep, Joe lifted his head and looked around. Then suddenly he sprang to his feet and burst into tears of joy. "FREE!" he shouted over and over again, running up and down the train like a madman and kissing anyone he could grab hold of. "FREE!" Then Joe ran over to Harriet, lifted her off her feet and spun her around.

"I'm free! Only one more journey left for me now, and that is to heaven!"

"Well you old fool," Harriet said, hiding her smile, "you might have looked at the Falls first and then gone to heaven afterwards!"

But back in the United States, heaven seemed further and further away as all hell was beginning to break loose over the issue of slavery . . .

"Kidnappers! Thieves!"

In Philadelphia and other northern cities, angry crowds of people shouted and blocked the way of slave catchers as they marched captured slaves through the streets. Rocks and glass were thrown, and blood was often shed. In Boston, huge signs were posted that read:

**Caution!! Colored People of Boston
You are hereby cautioned to avoid talking
to Police Officers
They have the legal right to act as
Kidnappers
Avoid them in every possible manner
They are Hounds on the track of the most
unfortunate of your race!**

Because the Fugitive Slave Law was a law, black people were no longer safe even around those who had once protected them. Hundreds and hundreds of black families had to run from their homes, their friends, and their professions and escape to Canada with nothing more than a sack of belongings . . .

"Any of y'all try to escape, I'll personally hunt you down and shoot you dead. If I ever even hear any of y'all talking about escape, you'll get forty lashes with the whip."

Throughout the South, slave owners tried in vain to scare slaves away from trying to escape. But threats, whippings, and torture did not keep slaves from running to Canada by the hundreds. As a result, slave owners became crueler. And though they would not admit it, slave owners were becoming afraid of their slaves. Every week, there was another story of a slave who stood up to his master, who grabbed the whip from his master's hand, who refused to be treated like property. In some parts of the South, slaves outnumbered white people. And like a distant thunder that was getting louder, slave owners could feel a storm brewing . . .

"There is not a nation on the earth guilty of practices more shocking and bloody than are the people of these United States at this very hour!"

Former slave Frederick Douglass shouted these words to a huge crowd of white people in Rochester, New York, on the Fourth of July. And the crowd cheered their approval. Douglass, an author and a famous speaker, had been invited by the mayor to speak about slavery. And Douglass did not hold back his burning anger.

"This Fourth of July is yours, not mine!" Douglass boomed, raising his fist into the air. For how could even one black person of the millions of black people in the United States celebrate Independence Day when not one black person was truly free?

And as the storm brewed, Harriet continued quietly leading slaves to freedom. By the late 1850s, she had helped more than 300 slaves to escape. Her name was now known around the world, but she shrugged off her own fame. Even so, more and more people who hated slavery were curious about this small, strong woman known to her people as "Moses." Again and again, Harriet was invited to speak at gatherings, but she always turned down the invitations.

"I can't read or write. I ain't ever given a speech. What would I have to say that would make a difference?" Harriet asked her friend William Still one afternoon when they were both in Boston.

"Everything you have to say would make a difference, Harriet," William said. "You have lived as a slave. You must tell people what that was like."

"But why? Everyone knows being a slave ain't a good life," Harriet responded.

"No, everyone doesn't know that. There are still people, even here in Boston, who believe that slaves are treated just fine. They think of black people as being like happy children who need a strong master to take care of them."

Harriet stared at William and shook her head. That night, she stood up before a large crowd at a safe gathering and spoke. Her voice started out quiet and low, but as the words came, her voice grew strong and confident:

"I grew up like a neglected weed—didn't know nothing about liberty, since I never had any. I was not happy; every time I seen a white man, I was afraid of being carried away. I've seen hundreds of escaped slaves, but I ain't never saw one who wanted to go back and be a slave. I think slavery is the next thing to hell!"

Late that night, Harriet was dreaming. It was the same dream she had dreamed for three nights in a row. In it, she was walking all alone through a wilderness in the mountains. Suddenly a huge snake raised its head from behind a rock and looked at her. As Harriet looked back, the snake's head turned into the head of an old man. The man had a long white beard and kind eyes. Harriet did not feel afraid. And it seemed as though the man was sad and trying to tell Harriet something important.

Suddenly, Harriet awoke. Outside, a wind was picking up and bending the branches of the trees. Harriet sat up in her bed—through her window, the North Star shone brightly. Harriet thought about her dream and could not understand what it meant; but she could feel something in her soul. Something was happening, something was moving. It was more than just the wind outside—the winds of change were beginning to build to hurricane force.

CHAPTER 8

On a cold spring morning in 1859, Harriet was traveling through Troy, New York, on yet another trip to rescue slaves. She was always in a hurry now—there was no time to waste. The disagreements about slavery were nearing a boiling point, and Harriet feared for the lives of all men, women, and children who were still slaves. However, Harriet rarely worried about her own life being in danger. And because of this, Harriet decided to make an unexpected stop in Troy.

"Watch out, grandma. You're in the way," a jailer snapped at the elderly black woman who was standing in a hallway near a jail cell. In the jail cell was a black man named Charles Nalle. He had been a hardworking, well-liked member of Troy's community. But out of the blue, a slave owner from Virginia showed up and demanded that Nalle be returned to him. Now Nalle was handcuffed in a jail cell as his master was signing papers.

Out in the street, an angry mob of about 600 people screamed and yelled for Nalle's release. Many were carrying knives, large sticks, and rocks.

"Let's buy him from his master!" someone shouted.

"I wouldn't pay that monster one cent! No one can own another human being!" someone else screamed back.

Ignoring the noise out in the street, the jailer opened Nalle's cell to lead him down the hall to his master. Suddenly, a window flew open and the elderly woman popped her head out.

"Here he comes! Grab him when he comes out!" she shouted out to the crowd, ripping off her old bonnet and shawl and standing up straight. Moses! Many in the crowd immediately recognized Harriet. In a flash, Harriet ran down the hall after the prisoner, fighting off one and then two police officers. Harriet grabbed Nalle tightly and tumbled out into the street with him.

The crowd immediately swarmed around Nalle and Harriet, trying to protect them from the law officers who were suddenly pouring out of the jail and other buildings nearby.

Policemen's clubs struck Harriet again and again, but she never let go of Nalle as they were pushed closer and closer to the Hudson River. By the time Harriet and Nalle reached a small boat that would carry them across the river, Harriet's clothes were torn from her, and her shoes had been pulled off. Both she and Nalle were bruised and bleeding.

Once across the river, Harriet thought Nalle was safe. But suddenly, a big sheriff with a pistol appeared. Harriet had no choice but to let go of Nalle. Within minutes, however, the angry crowd had crossed the river and was banging on the door and breaking the windows of the office where Nalle was being held. Gunshots rang out and rocks were hurled through the air. In the struggle, one man was killed with a hatchet thrown by the deputy. But in the end, Harriet carried Nalle out to the street where he was taken by carriage to Canada. Then, wrapped in a blanket, Harriet quietly slipped out of town to continue her work.

Meanwhile, halfway across the United States, in Kansas, a white man named John Brown had heard about Harriet Tubman. Brown believed that the only way to handle slave owners was to fight them—brutally. The time for talk and laws and patience was over. Brown wanted to attack the plantations in the

South and attack them with such a bloody fury that the slave owners wouldn't know what had hit them. And John Brown knew the perfect person to help him plan the attacks—Moses.

"Slavery is a state of war!" Brown exclaimed as he sat in Harriet's kitchen in her little house in St. Catharine's. Brown had traveled to meet with Harriet and discuss his battle plans.

"We will gather slaves and white men who want to fight, and we will hide in the mountains. There, we will train and prepare. And when the time is right . . . " Brown stared at Harriet, his old eyes shining. Harriet stared back. Had she already met this man? He seemed so familiar, and yet . . .

Her dream! The snake with the head of an old man with a long white beard—it was John Brown. Harriet still could not understand what the dream meant, but she knew she must work with Brown and help him. She was convinced that her dreams and visions were sent by God.

"Just tell me what you need me to do," Harriet said quietly.

"I need you to help me lead my forces . . . *General* Tubman," Brown answered seriously. And from that point on, Brown always referred to Harriet as "General." Although Brown did not think women should be involved in wars and battles, Harriet was an exception. In her, he saw more strength and bravery than he'd ever seen in most men.

For months, Harriet and Brown planned, stared at maps, and gathered guns and soldiers. Hundreds of "pikes" were made—long poles with sharp ends that the soldiers would use in battle. Finally, Brown rented an old farmhouse in Harper's Ferry, Virginia, as his headquarters. He began counting down the days until he, General Tubman, and the soldiers would begin their attacks.

But on the first day of John Brown's battle plan, Harriet was too sick to fight. She had never stopped her Underground Railroad work, even as she and Brown planned for battle. After a particularly cold and long journey, Harriet had become quite ill. And now, as Brown and his soldiers marched into their first attack near Harper's Ferry, Harriet could only lie in bed and wait for the news. Finally the news came.

"Oh no." William Still, who was visiting his sick friend, was staring at a newspaper and shaking his head. Harriet glared at him, thinking back all those years ago to when Zeke would read bad news to himself and shake his head while his cabin was full of slaves waiting to hear the news.

"What?" Harriet asked impatiently, wishing for the thousandth time that she could read.

"Attack at Harper's Ferry," William read.

"Slave uprising led by Kansan John Brown. President Buchanan calls out Marines and Cavalry as Colonel Robert E. Lee leads the attack on John Brown and his men."

William paused and looked at Harriet sadly. "Well, is that it?" Harriet asked. "Are they still fighting?"

William sighed and continued reading: "John Brown captured. Taken to Charleston, South Carolina, to be hanged."

Harriet put her head in her hands for several minutes. Then she looked over at William. "This is just the beginning," she said angrily. "John always said 'Slavery is a state of war.' Now the war's begun."

"We don't have to be part of this country! I say we form our own new nation!" A slave owner in South Carolina pounded his fist on the table as he spoke to a crowd of hundreds.

"Abe Lincoln can't tell us what to do," another man yelled from the crowd. "Ain't no new president gonna force us to give up our slaves—our property!"

Throughout the South, state after state began announcing that it no longer wanted to be part of the United States. Instead, a group of Southern states formed "The Confederate States of America" and even elected their own president.

Meanwhile, President Lincoln paced the floors of the Capitol in Washington, D.C. He could not allow states to just decide that they no longer wanted to be a part of this country; that was against the law. He had no choice but to send troops down South to try and settle things down.

"We must not be enemies," Lincoln said in one of his first speeches as president. But one month later, the roar of cannons and guns filled the air in Charleston, South Carolina.

Harriet's days as a conductor on the Underground Railroad were suddenly over. With a war raging along the very paths and through the very woods she used to travel, it was much too dangerous for her to try and help slaves escape anymore. But Harriet worried. What would happen to all the slaves in the South if the North didn't win the war? Like Lincoln, Harriet paced the floors. And soon she began to grow restless.

"Don't know how or where, but I'm gonna join the Yankee army," Harriet calmly announced during breakfast one morning. She was spending some time with her parents in St. Catharine's.

"What!?" Rit stared at her daughter for a moment and then looked desperately at Ben. But Ben just smiled and shook his head.

"Now Hat," Rit began, "you've done all you can do, and I . . . "

"All I can do?" Harriet asked with a little surprised laugh. "I won't have done all I can do until the war is over and every slave is free."

"Well, you might as well give up your foolish notion," Rit said firmly, "because they don't let no women be soldiers."

Harriet sat for a while staring out the house's front door. Finally she stood up, stretched, and went over and put her hand on her mother's shoulder. "Ma," she said gently. "They'll let me."

Within the year, Harriet stood on the deck of the *U.S.S Atlantic* as it approached the shores of South Carolina. Before her were strange sounds and sights she had never experienced before. The constant boom of cannons rumbled like thunder as trails of smoke filled the skies. Along the shore, palmetto trees swayed in a hot and sticky spring breeze. And swimming beside the ship were chattering porpoises and schools of shiny little fish.

Harriet had been asked to come to Beaufort, South Carolina, to help the thousands of slaves along the South Carolina and Georgia shores who had been left behind by their masters. Their masters had packed bags quickly and run away in terror when they heard the guns of the

Yankee armies approaching. And many of the slaves were left without food or water.

"You have quite a difficult job to do, Harriet," said General Hunter, the army officer who gave Harriet her orders. He had come out on deck to stand beside Harriet.

"Won't be so hard, sir," Harriet said with a shrug. "They're my people. I been helping them for years now."

"Well," said General Hunter, looking at Harriet carefully. "This is different. The slaves here are . . . " he scratched his head as he thought of the right way to say it. "Well, some of them may be afraid of you."

"Afraid? Why, all my people know Moses gonna help them, not hurt them."

"That's just it, Harriet," the general explained. "None of these slaves have ever heard of you. For generations, they have lived on island plantations along the coast. They don't know anything beyond their own little islands—not the war, not the Underground Railroad, and not Moses. Many of them don't even speak English."

Harriet gave the general a funny look. "Don't speak English, sir? How am I gonna talk with them then?"

"That, Harriet, is part of what I meant by 'difficult,'" General Hunter said with a small smile.

As the ship moved beyond the coastline and in along the waterways through the islands, Harriet saw more strange sights. Rice fields stretched out into the water, and through them slid alligators. Past the rice fields were huge oak trees with weird gray moss hanging from them. And behind the trees, giant, white plantation houses stood deserted. Often, their front doors were open, and leaves blew in and out of the doorways. Every so often, Harriet would see black people peeping around trees at the ship. More than once, she saw tall black women with baskets on their heads grab their children and run away into the shadows.

Finally, the ship pulled into the harbor at Beaufort. Harriet looked down into the small town's streets and was stunned. For as far as she could see, black people sat, stood, leaned or walked slowly. Many were being tended to by soldiers or nurses. Every doorstep was filled with black children. Many looked happy and busy, but just as many looked frightened and sick.

"Your job will involve nursing many of these people back to health," General Hunter instructed as he and Harriet walked onto the docks. "Also, you will be helping the women to learn new skills. They're going to need to know how to earn some money once they leave here."

"But . . . " Harriet began, bewildered. "How did so many get here?"

"Many who were sick or starving found their way here. Others have been coaxed onto rescue boats and brought here. Some have already been here a year or longer, so they've got a head start." General Hunter stopped walking and looked around, shaking his head.

"Harriet, we figure there may be close to 10,000 slaves here and in the nearby islands. Nearly all of them need help in some way." The General turned to look at Harriet, and then he smiled. "We are so glad you're here. I wish we had about a hundred Harriet Tubmans to help us!"

As Harriet wandered into the hot, busy streets, several black children ran over to her and grabbed her hands excitedly.

"We're free! We're free!" shouted one little boy who looked to be about eight years old. He was very thin with dust in his hair, and his shorts were muddy and tattered. But Harriet noticed he was holding a small book. She stooped down to look directly at the little boy.

"That your book, son?" she asked.

"Yessum," the boy nodded happily. "They's teaching us to read words. Look!" The boy pulled Harriet over to a bench and sat close to her and opened up his book.

"The . . . sky . . . is . . . b-b-blue!" He read slowly and then grinned widely up at Harriet. Harriet put her arm around the little boy and hugged him tightly. *You're free all right,* she thought as she fought back happy tears.

CHAPTER 9

"I'm sorry, Harriet. We just can't pay you," General Hunter said with a sigh one evening. "That's President Lincoln's orders. No pay for black soldiers or nurses yet. But you'll get your pay soon."

"But sir, y'all been saying 'soon' for a half year now," Harriet said.

"Well, the best we can do for now is to keep giving you meals and a place to live."

Harriet was silent. For months now, she had been giving many of her meals to the frightened slave women who came to Beaufort from the islands. It was one of the few ways she could win their trust. General Hunter had been right—many of the island slaves were afraid to speak to the white people who were trying to help them. And they weren't sure about Harriet either since she worked with the white people.

But over time, through food and sometimes song sharing, Harriet became their friend.

"But it ain't right," Harriet finally continued. "Black men aim their rifles and spill their blood the same as white men. And I clean up the blood and put on bandages same as a white woman."

General Hunter looked out his window at the all-black group of soldiers training in the hot sun. It had taken nearly a year to convince Lincoln that the Yankee army should allow black men to fight in this war too. Now the government was reluctant to pay them. This made General Hunter as angry as it made Harriet.

"No, it's not right," the General said, turning back to Harriet. "It's shameful."

But Harriet was not one to complain or to sit around worrying. She went home to her small cabin that evening and did what she had been doing for several months. Pulling sacks of flour and sugar and other ingredients out of her cupboard, Harriet began making the dozens of pies and gingerbread cookies that she would sell to hungry white soldiers the next day. In this way, Harriet made enough money to feed herself and even buy extra food for the starving, frightened island slaves who arrived every day. But she was often up past midnight baking.

At the crack of dawn the next day, Harriet was out the door and off to tend to wounded soldiers and sick slaves in the hospital. Every morning, it was the same routine. Harriet would take a big chunk of ice and put it in a bowl of water. Then she would sponge the soldiers' wounds until the ice had all melted, and the bowl was red with their blood. Many of the wounds were infected and attracted so many flies that Harriet spent half her time swatting flies away from the men.

Other patients had drunk bad water and were very sick with a disease called dysentery. Before Harriet had arrived, many soldiers and slaves had been dying from this illness. But Harriet knew of a tea she could make from roots and plants that seemed to cure dysentery. So, every day at noon, Harriet would follow a path deep into a swamp and dig up mysterious roots. Then she would boil the roots and plants, pour the tea into jars, and head back to the hospital with her potion.

Harriet's afternoons were spent showing the slave women how to do jobs that might earn them a living some day. From her years of odd jobs in Philadelphia, Harriet knew a number of skills. But most of these women and girls knew nothing more than how to chop cotton or gather rice. However, it wasn't always easy for Harriet to explain things to them.

"They laugh and laugh when they hear me talk, sir," Harriet said to General Hunter one afternoon. "They think it's me who's talking funny!"

"Yes," the general agreed. "It's an unusual language they speak."

"Parts of it English, and parts some other kind of words I can't understand," Harriet said thoughtfully. "Still, they know all the same songs I know. Why, we all sing and sing together, and the next thing I know, it ain't so hard to understand each other anymore."

One cool November morning as Harriet was hurrying to the hospital as usual, General Hunter stopped her.

"Harriet, we are going to have a new job for you in a couple months."

"A new job?" Harriet asked slowly, not sure what he meant.

"Wonderful news has come from Washington," the general said with a smile. "Two months from now, on January 1st, Mr. Lincoln will sign a law that puts an end to slavery forever. Slavery will no longer be legal in any state—every black man, woman, and child will be free!"

Harriet stared at the general for a moment and then suddenly grasped his hands. "Truly free? We're really all free?"

"Well, not quite yet. But, yes, on January 1st, 1863, slavery will end."

Harriet felt as though she could do a little dance right there in the street, but she pulled herself together quickly.

"And what job do you need me to do now, sir?"

"Well, it's going to be a bit more dangerous," he said, looking at Harriet carefully.

"I've known danger before, sir," Harriet said.

"Yes, I certainly know that, Harriet. That's why you've been chosen for this special job. Let me explain . . . "

As Harriet and General Hunter walked through the morning streets of Beaufort, the general told Harriet the new plans. She would be traveling on gunboats much further inland along with Colonel Montgomery and a few hundred soldiers. All along the rivers where they'd be traveling were enemy camps. Hundreds or even thousands of Rebel soldiers were hidden in abandoned plantations or old barns.

"You see," the general explained, "there will still be hundreds of slaves who won't even know they're free. The Rebels certainly won't let them know about the new law. Part of your job will be letting them know they're free." Here, the general paused and took a deep breath. "Plus, Harriet, these slaves would be afraid to speak to a white soldier . . . but they'll talk to you."

"Talk to me, sir? About what?" Harriet asked.

"About where the Rebel troops are," the general said quietly. "About where torpedoes in the river are hidden. About the bridges that have armed guards."

General Hunter stopped and put his hand on Harriet's shoulder.

"You're going to need to travel ahead of the gunboats on foot and find these slaves and get information from them. Also, of course, let them know they're free. Then you will return to the boats and let Colonel Montgomery know what's ahead."

"Yes sir," Harriet said with no fear whatsoever in her voice.

"Harriet, we're asking you to be a spy. This is a very dangerous job, because if you get caught . . . "

Harriet smiled proudly as she spoke the words she had spoken so often during her years as a conductor on the Underground Railroad: "They won't ever catch me. Never!"

Several months later, Harriet was dressed in a blue uniform and she carried a rifle over her shoulder as she crept several miles through the moonlit woods. This was a different kind of woods than what she had known up north. Huge bugs flew into her face, and more than once, a snake slithered across her path. Strange sounds rattled, hooted, and snapped all around her. But not far ahead, Harriet could see the glow of fires and hear low voices. Straining her eyes, Harriet could make out two black men sitting on the steps of a cabin. As she crept closer, Harriet began singing low so as not to startle the men.

"Who's there?" the older man asked, standing up.

"A friend," Harriet said. "Don't be scared." But as Harriet walked out of the woods in her uniform, with her gun, both men jumped back in alarm. Harriet motioned for them to sit down and quietly explained who she was and what she was doing.

"Are you . . . " the younger man leaned close to Harriet and looked at her. "Are you the one they call Moses?"

Within minutes, the whispered name had blazed through the slaves' quarters, and dozens of slaves ran out to see Harriet—and to share what they knew.

"Just up the river a mile, you'll pass a big old house. Inside is all the guns and ammunition for the Rebel troops in this area. I know 'cause it used to be my master's house an' the Rebel soldiers made me move the guns inside," said one.

"But watch out for guards. They hide behind the three big magnolia trees in front of the house," said another. "Three guards behind each tree."

"And look here," an old woman said as she walked near the firelight. "I can draw you a map to the next Big House on up fifteen miles or so. I hear tell that's where a couple hundred or more soldiers is camped out."

In this way, Harriet gained all the information the Yankee troops on the gunboats needed to proceed. And before she left the slaves, she told them the news they hadn't heard.

"Y'all are free, now!" Harriet shouted joyfully to the group. "President Lincoln done signed it into law. Gather your things, and we'll pick y'all up along the river on our way back to Beaufort."

This news was greeted with tears of joy, laughter, and shouting. Although they had days to get ready, many slaves scattered and ran as fast as they could to start throwing pots, pans, shoes, food, and anything else they owned into big burlap sacks.

"Ain't never got a chance to ride that Railroad," shouted one elderly man as he hobbled quickly to his cabin. "Sure ain't gonna miss that boat!"

As Harriet sneaked through the woods and along the river's edge back to the gunboats, she could hear the singing of the slaves growing fainter and fainter. The only light coming from the boats was the glow of Colonel Montgomery's pipe as he waited silently for Harriet's return. Although there were hundreds of soldiers preparing for battle onboard, the boats were deathly quiet.

"Got the information we need," Harriet whispered as she was helped aboard. She and Colonel Montgomery sat close together and spoke quietly for a short time. Then the colonel gave the quiet command for the boats to begin moving further up the river toward the plantation where guns and ammunition were stored.

Fifty Yankee soldiers silently moved onshore and crept through the woods. Because of Harriet's help, they knew which trees the Rebel guards would be stationed behind. Tiptoeing in the dark with their rifles aimed, the Yankee soldiers took all of the Rebel guards by complete surprise. Then, in a flash of light, soldiers set the old plantation house on fire. Hundreds and hundreds of guns and thousands of pounds of ammunition went up in flames in the night. Harriet stood on the deck of one of the gunboats and watched the eerie sight of the plantation house burning down. Suddenly, an old memory of a seven-year-old slave girl who was whipped for not knowing how to dust the furniture inside a house like this one came back to Harriet. Harriet was not sad to see the house crumble to the ground in ashes.

Fifteen miles up the river, 200 Rebel soldiers were sound asleep. As the gunboats moved closer and closer, Colonel Montgomery spoke quietly to his soldiers.

"Men, Harriet Tubman has acquired information about the compound we are preparing to attack. Nearly 200 Rebels are camped out in this location. If we move quietly and swiftly, we should be able to overtake them."

As the colonel spoke, Harriet looked around at the faces of the young men. All were brave, but some were afraid. Although this would be a surprise attack, Harriet knew that many of these men would die in the battle. When the boats reached the old plantation, all of the soldiers slipped off and disappeared quietly into the woods surrounding the Big House. There was a short time of utter silence, and then some yells, and then the battle began. Years later, Harriet described that night to a friend:

"We saw the lightning, and that was the guns. And then we heard the thunder and that was the big guns. And then we heard the rain falling and that was the blood falling. And when we came in to get the crops, it was dead men that we reaped."

In this way, the gunboats continued up the river, surprising camps and guarded supply stores and winning battle after battle. General Hunter had been right; Harriet proved to be an excellent spy and scout. She always got her information—and she never got caught.

On the return trip to Beaufort, Harriet was amazed by the number of slaves lining the riverbanks. Baskets on their heads, children on their shoulders, and everything from chickens to chairs in sacks on their backs, the slaves cheered and waved as the boats approached. These were the slaves who had led the most difficult lives in the "down South" that Harriet had always feared. And these were the last slaves to have learned that they were free. On their faces were lines from worry and scars from beatings. But as Harriet looked at the hundreds of faces along the banks, she didn't see one that wasn't smiling.

CHAPTER 10

"From what I can figure, the government owes me nearly $2,000."

Harriet was sitting at her kitchen table looking over scraps of paper and official documents. Her parents, Ben and Rit, had moved in with Harriet in an old farmhouse in Auburn, New York. After nearly two years of serving as an Army nurse and spy, Harriet had been sent home for time off and rest.

"Well, they ain't paid you a penny yet, and the war's almost over!" Rit exclaimed with a disgusted sigh.

It was true—Harriet had never seen any pay for all of her hard work. Promises and slips of paper showing what she was owed were all Harriet had.

"But these papers here are from the government," Harriet said with a frown. "They say that I'm gonna get paid, so I believe my pay will come."

Rit snorted a little laugh. "You can believe what you want, but I reckon the government is gonna keep sending you slips of paper with promises until you give up trying to get that pay."

Ben had been sitting and quietly listening to his wife and daughter.

"How much you say the black soldiers are finally getting paid?" he asked.

"Seven dollars a month," Harriet answered.

"And what do white soldiers get?" asked Ben.

"About fourteen dollars a month," Harriet said quietly.

Ben scratched his head and thought for a few minutes. "Seems to me that the government thinks a black man is only worth half what a white man's worth. Reckon they don't think a black woman's worth no pay at all."

"But I got papers that say . . . " Harriet began.

"Don't make no difference," Ben said. "We black folks all got our freedom now, but things ain't gonna be fair for us for a long time, Hat. Everything don't change overnight."

Harriet stared at her papers and promises. She still believed that the country she had served would treat her with respect and fairness. But deep in her heart, she wondered—was her father right?

Harriet had barely had enough time to catch her breath, much less rest, when she received an official letter from the Army. Her help was needed in a hospital near Washington, D.C.

"Now, Hat, you should tell 'em you ain't going nowhere until you get paid first," Rit said angrily.

"But that's just it, Ma," Harriet said, pointing to the letter that a neighbor had read to her. "The Army says I need to come back and do this last job in order to get paid. Plus, the work is in an all-black hospital. They need me."

Rit just shook her head. "I 'spect the government always needs people who will work hard for free."

But Harriet packed her bags and boarded the first train for Washington. It was not in her nature to turn her back on people who needed her just because she wasn't getting paid. *Ain't no one in the Old Testament ever paid Moses to help his people!* Harriet thought as she stared out the train window. But even so, Harriet was troubled. Her parents were getting old now and required more care.

How would she afford to take care of them if the money never came through?

Finally, Harriet reached the hospital for black soldiers and freed slaves. When she walked in the front door, the stink of sickness and filth nearly knocked her over. Everywhere she looked, patients were poorly attended to—they were dirty, their bandages were old, their stitches were infected. Small children huddled beneath the beds of their parents, looking frightened or sick. Flies and even birds flew in and out of broken windows. Harriet was stunned and furious. *Wouldn't be like this if there was white soldiers here,* she thought.

However, Harriet wasted little time on being angry. Immediately, she went out into the streets and began asking black men and women to help her. In just a few days, Harriet had assembled her own army of workers who scrubbed, swept, re-painted, and re-bandaged. Harriet personally walked into government offices in Washington, D.C., and demanded more doctors and better medicine for the dying soldiers who had fought so bravely.

Meanwhile, the war was coming to an end. Harriet had always dreamed of the day when the U.S. flag would be raised over Southern cities again. She had long looked forward to being at the victory celebrations in Charleston and Beaufort. But on the evening that the

Stars and Stripes were raised over Charleston, Harriet was scrubbing bathroom floors in the hospital. The night that the Yankee forces declared victory and huge parties were thrown in Beaufort, Harriet was up until 3:00 a.m. soothing a soldier who had lost both legs.

Finally, there was nothing left to be done. The war was over, the hospital Harriet had been assigned to was in order, and Harriet was told she could go home for good. As always, she was given a slip of paper that promised to pay her—some day. But she was also given a special ticket to ride in a first-class car on the train back home. It wasn't much, but Harriet was proud of the ticket and the honor.

As Harriet settled into her seat, she noticed that the train car she was in suddenly became very quiet. Several people were staring at her with annoyed expressions. Within minutes, the train's conductor rushed over to her.

"Girl, you can't sit in this car," the conductor said loudly as he reached for Harriet's arm to lift her out of the seat.

Embarrassed and confused, Harriet pulled out her special ticket. "But, sir, I have this paper here that says . . . "

"I don't care about no piece of paper!" the conductor barked angrily. "No black people are allowed in this car—you people sit in the back.

Now move!"

But Harriet had reached her limit. "No sir. I will not move," Harriet said calmly, looking straight ahead.

"Oh, you'll move all right," the conductor said with a sneer as he grabbed Harriet by the shoulder and yanked her out of the seat. Still, Harriet tried to sit back down. Then other passengers joined in to help the conductor pull Harriet out of her seat. Eventually, it took four men to throw Harriet into the baggage car near the back of the train.

"You stupid, stubborn old fool! Don't you know your place?" the conductor shouted as he slammed the door of the baggage car.

Harriet lay in the dark with a badly injured shoulder as the train moved through Washington and on toward her home in New York. For many miles, her father's words rushed over and over again in her head: *Things ain't gonna be fair for us for a long time*. Now she no longer wondered—she knew that what her father had said was true.

When Harriet returned to her new home in Auburn, Rit took one look at her and knew that her daughter needed rest. Harriet was only forty-five, but she looked nearly as old as her mother after so many years of exhausting work.

"You gonna sit on that front porch and just

watch the world go on by now," Rit said. "Let everyone else take care of you for a while."

Harriet nodded and sat down, happy to finally have some time to spend with her aging parents. She sat on the porch sipping lemonade while Ben and Rit fixed up the farmhouse and planted a garden in the backyard. Neighbors, friends, and fans of Harriet's work came to visit, and many of them brought food and money to help Harriet and her parents. Although Harriet never publicly complained, many people had heard about how the government had never paid Harriet one cent for all her work.

Black, white, rich, and poor—a constant stream of well-wishers found their way to the old farmhouse in Auburn. Once, a young lawyer from Washington showed up. He had been a passenger on the train when Harriet was thrown out of her seat and injured.

"I'd be glad to represent you in court," he said to Harriet. "You have a very good case for a lawsuit that could bring you a lot of money." But Harriet just smiled and shook her head no. That wasn't the way she wanted to earn money.

It wasn't long before Harriet grew tired of being taken care of. Her old instinct for taking care of others was slowly revving up again. One afternoon, a very poor, young mother with a sick daughter showed up at Harriet's door. The

HARRIET TUBMAN: FREEDOM LEADER **111**

mother was trying to sell eggs to make a little money to buy medicine for her child. Harriet invited them in for tea, and within a couple hours she had moved them into a small spare room upstairs.

Soon, Harriet's home gained a reputation as being a place where the poor, sick, or elderly could go for help and comfort. Harriet began working hard at her old jobs of cooking, cleaning, and baking pies and cookies in order to bring in enough money to take care of her parents and guests.

"You just beat all, Hat," Rit would say, trying to look angry while hiding her smile. "Reckon you'd be miserable if you couldn't be working yourself to death."

"Reckon so," Harriet said with a wink as she hugged her old mother.

One spring morning, a different kind of visitor showed up.

"Miss Tubman?" A tall, handsome black man stood at Harriet's front door smiling shyly.

"Yes sir," Harriet replied, looking at him curiously.

"Bet you don't remember me, do you?" he asked.

Harriet seemed to recognize something in his smile, but she couldn't quite place his face.

"We met back in Beaufort when I was

training with the all-black regiment. I remember being so honored to meet you!" The young man's eyes twinkled as he reached out his hand. "I'm Nelson Davis."

Harriet shook his hand and welcomed him into her home. Their conversation and memories of Beaufort stretched out into the afternoon and then into the evening. Harriet learned that though Nelson appeared healthy, he was sick with a disease called tuberculosis. Immediately, Harriet offered to care for Nelson and give him a place to live if he needed it.

"No, I couldn't trouble you for that," Nelson said sincerely, shaking his head.

"Ain't any trouble. It'd do my heart good to help out a soldier," Harriet replied.

"Well . . . maybe just a few days," Nelson agreed slowly.

But a few days became a few weeks, which soon became a few months. Before long, Nelson had become a regular member of the household, and Harriet loved his company and his twinkling eyes. One year after he had shown up at Harriet's door, Nelson and Harriet were married in the Central Church of Auburn. Harriet was nearly fifty, and Nelson was thirty, but everyone at the wedding could see how they loved and admired each other.

•   •   •

Many years of peace and happiness followed. Harriet cared tenderly for her parents in their final years. She spent many hours in the large flower and vegetable garden behind her house, growing much of the food she needed. And she and Nelson continued to welcome the elderly, the poor, or the sick into their home.

One day, a young woman named Sarah Bradford came to visit Harriet—but she was not seeking help from Harriet; she wanted to give help to her. Sarah had heard many amazing stories about Harriet Tubman through the years, and she decided that if these stories were actually true, she would like to write a book about Harriet.

"Miss Tubman, I'd like to tell the story of your life," Sarah explained over coffee one afternoon. "And if it sells well, you can pay off your house with the money it brings in."

Harriet wasn't sure. She was not always comfortable talking about herself. But she did believe that it was important to talk about the Underground Railroad and the Civil War. Plus, she was always scraping money together to try and make house payments. More than once, the bank had even threatened to take her home away from her.

"Well, Miss Bradford, on my Underground Railroad I never ran my train off the track and I never lost a passenger, so I 'spose I have a story to tell," Harriet finally responded.

Harriet and Sarah talked and talked for many days. Some of the stories that Harriet told seemed almost impossible, but Sarah believed her.

"No one can hear Harriet talk," she later told a friend, " and not believe every word she says."

The book, *Scenes in the Life of Harriet Tubman,* was a huge success. People around the world read it and were thrilled by the life and strength of this tiny woman who had been born a slave and beaten all the odds, risked her life, and fought in a war. True to her promise, Sarah Bradford gave much of the money from the sales of the book to Harriet. In fact, it was enough money for Harriet to both pay off her own home and also buy another house next door to hers.

"All my guests done outgrown one house," Harriet explained. So in 1908, the Harriet Tubman Home for Aged and Indigent Negroes opened its doors to more needy people.

In this way, giving and caring for others, Harriet grew into her seventies and then into her eighties. As an old woman, she went to the funerals of many of her friends: William Still, Frederick Douglass, and her old stationmaster friend, Thomas Garrett. Even her young husband, finally worn down by tuberculosis, died before Harriet. But Harriet was forever surrounded by friends and family members who loved her for all the sacrifices she had made.

On a chilly morning in 1912, Harriet sat in church listening to the music she had always loved. But when it was over, she grasped the hand of a friend sitting near her.

"I can hear them bells a-ringing," she whispered. "I can hear the angels singing. I can see the hosts a-marching."

Harriet knew. As she had so often seen visions throughout her long life, her last vision was one of her own life ending. And not long after this vision, Harriet became very sick. Friends gathered around her bedside quietly, holding her hands and reading her favorite stories from the Bible. Finally, one evening just as the stars were coming out, Harriet whispered for her favorite song to be sung.

As Harriet Tubman closed her eyes for the last time, every voice in the room raised the glorious song. And after years of riding the Underground Railroad, hiding in broken-down wagons, and being forced to back seats on trains, Harriet would finally ride home in style:

She died in 1913 not 1912

Swing Low, Sweet Chariot
Coming for to Carry Me Home!

AFTERWORD

The book you have just read is a true story about a real person. Harriet Tubman's life and work were so amazing that many books, called "biographies," have been written about her. Some of these books about Tubman are historical fact. This means that everything in the biography is a fact from history and nothing has been made up for the sake of storytelling. Other biographies, like this one, are historical fiction. This means that some of the things, such as conversations, descriptions, and even the thoughts that Harriet was thinking, are made up—they're fiction.

You might wonder why a biography about Harriet Tubman would contain fiction. There are a couple reasons why. First of all, Harriet lived long before anything could be recorded or filmed. Therefore, we don't really know how she spoke or exactly what she might have said. We have to make a good guess based on her actions. Also, Harriet could not write, so we have very few records of exactly how she felt about certain things. But, once again, we can be pretty sure of how she felt based on the things she did.

Even so, we do have Sarah Bradford's helpful book, *Scenes From the Life of Harriet Tubman,* which is full of quotes from Harriet. Bradford's book also contains a lot of letters from friends of Harriet's. These letters let us know that all the incredible stories about the things that Harriet did during her life are true. Plus, we have old newspaper stories about Harriet that give us the facts about her travels, work, and many sacrifices.

So, while some of the conversations and descriptions in this book you've just read are made up, all of the events and people are real. Harriet *did* lead 300 slaves to freedom on the Underground Railroad. She *did* fall asleep under her own "Wanted" poster. She *did* serve as a spy in the Civil War. And, yes, she really *did* hide from her master in a pigpen when she was seven years old.

One final real event involving Harriet Tubman took place in 2002—nearly ninety years after she died. A group of middle school students in Albany, New York, were reading and studying about Harriet. Like many people who have learned about Harriet, these students were shocked and angry to find out that the government had never paid her for her years of work in the Army. So, these students decided to do some more investigating.

They found out that Harriet did, in fact, receive some money from the government. But this was money she received only after her second husband, Nelson Davis, died. Davis had been a soldier in the Civil War, so his widow, Harriet, was to be paid a widow's pension of $25 per month. The government was still not willing to pay Harriet for her work, but at least she received a full widow's pension.

Or did she? The group of students did some more research. They found out that Harriet was actually only paid $20 a month! For the last fourteen years of her life, Harriet was cheated out of five dollars a month. The students decided to take some action to make things right. They met with their state senator, Senator Hillary Clinton, and told her about how unfairly Harriet had been treated. They felt that Harriet's relatives living today should receive the money that Harriet was never paid.

Senator Clinton brought the matter to the attention of the U.S. Senate and requested that $11,750 be paid to Harriet's relatives. This was the amount of money Harriet was owed, adjusted to the amount it would be today.

Several months later, the money was paid to Harriet's relatives. But the relatives chose not to keep the money for themselves. Instead, they have donated it to the Harriet Tubman House and Museum in Auburn, New York.

We can only imagine that Harriet would be proud of the spirit of giving and selflessness that her relatives have kept alive.